A SHORT HISTORY OF IRELAND

RICHARD KILLEEN

GILL & MACMILLAN

FOR MY MOTHER

Text: Richard Killeen

Editor: Fleur Robertson

Editorial Assistance: Kirsty Wheeler

Design: Phillip Clucas

Photography: Australian Overseas Information Service, London; British Museum, London: CLB Publishing, Godalming; Cork Public Museum; Crawford Municipal Art Gallery, Cork; Derek Speirs/Report, Dublin; G.A. Duncan, Dublin; Gill & Macmillan, Dublin; Hulton Deutsch Picture Library, London; Irish Tourist Board, Dublin; Mansell Collection, London; Mary Evans Picture Library, London; Michael Diggin Photography, Tralee; National Gallery of Ireland, Dublin; National Gallery of London; National Library of Ireland, Dublin; National Museum of Ireland, Dublin; Office of Public Works, Dublin; The Slide File, Dublin; Billy Stickland; Trinity College Dublin; Ulster Museum, Belfast

Map: MicroMap, Romsey

Production: Ruth Arthur, Sally Connolly, Neil Randles, Jonathan Tickner

Director of Production: Gerald Hughes

Published in Ireland by Gill & Macmillan Ltd, Goldenbridge, Dublin 8 with associated companies throughout the world CLB 3422 ©1994 CLB Publishing, Godalming, Surrey, England ISBN 0 7171 2156 9 Printed and bound in Singapore

CONTENTS

INTRODUCTION

This short book is intended as an introduction to the history of Ireland for visitors and non-specialists. It assumes no previous knowledge of the subject.

Although a small country, Ireland has made a distinctive and lasting contribution to our world. For most of its history, it has been relatively isolated: in common with many other peripheral corners of Europe, it was never part of the Roman Empire. In medieval times, it was at best an autonomous region at the margin of English royal power; in fact, many areas lay outside the ambit of that power altogether.

From the sixteenth to the eighteenth centuries, Ireland gradually moved to being an English colony. In the nineteenth, it was wholly absorbed into the British state as an integral part of the United Kingdom. In the twentieth, most of the island has secured its independence and is now a full member state of the European Community.

The north-eastern corner has, however, chosen to remain within the United Kingdom. Northern Ireland, unlike the independent republic to the South, has a population which is divided in its national allegiances. That division has resulted in many years of bitter sectarian violence. Of all the questions posed about Irish history, that which asks how the present instability in Northern Ireland came into being is the one most often raised. I hope that this book will provide at least part of the answer.

Richard Killeen
February 1994

IRELAND
showing principal administrative divisions, towns and historic battle sites

Derry
LONDONDERRY
Ballymena
ANTRIM
DONEGAL
Strabane
ULSTER
Donegal
NORTHERN IRELAND
Belfast
Omagh
R Erne
TYRONE
DOWN
FERMANAGH
Armagh
Downpatrick
Sligo
Enniskillen
Monaghan
ARMAGH
Newry
MONAGHAN
LEITRIM
SLIGO
Cavan
Dundalk
MAYO
CAVAN
LOUTH
Achill Is
Castlebar
ROSCOMMON
LONGFORD
Longford
Navan
1690 Boyne
Roscommon
MEATH
CONNACHT
R Boyne
DUBLIN
Mullingar
WESTMEATH
GALWAY
Athlone
R Liffey
Dublin
1014 Clontarf
Galway
Ballinasloe
Tullamore
1691 Aughrim
OFFALY
KILDARE
Kildare
LEINSTER
R Shannon
Port Laoise
R Barrow
WICKLOW
Wicklow
Aran Islands
LAOIS
CLARE
REPUBLIC OF IRELAND
Ennis
Carlow
Thurles
CARLOW
R Nore
Limerick
Kilkenny
TIPPERARY
KILKENNY
WEXFORD
LIMERICK
Tipperary
1798 Vinegar Hill
Clonmel
Tralee
R Suir
Wexford
MUNSTER
Waterford
Killarney
R Blackwater
WATERFORD
KERRY
CORK
Cork
R Lee
1601 Kinsale

| 0 | | 20 | | 40 miles |
| 0 | 20 | 40 | | 60 km |

ised on the Ordnance Survey by permission of the Government (Permit No. 5813)

1. PRE-CELTIC IRELAND

Ireland was first inhabited around 7500 B.C. by settlers who probably came from Scotland to what is now Co. Antrim. These early Mesolithic (Middle Stone Age) people were primitive hunters and fishermen. They settled the coasts and the bigger river valleys, especially in the northern half of the island, although archaeological remains of their settlements have been found as far south as Co. Cork. However, the most extraordinary Mesolithic site is at Mount Sandel, Co. Derry, which has been dated to 5935 B.C. Its excavated structures are the oldest discovered human habitations in Europe.

Around 3500 B.C. the Mesolithic people were superseded by a new wave of settlers. Once again, these Neolithic (New Stone Age) people probably came from Scotland, making the short sea crossing from Argyll. They brought a priceless new skill: agriculture. The ability to cultivate land enabled them to outstrip the hunter-gatherers and establish permanent settlements. Their coming marks the beginning of civilised life in Ireland.

Evidence for the existence of Neolithic agriculture may be found at numerous archaeological sites throughout the island, but none is more extensive or as impressive as that at Belderg, Co. Mayo, which dates from the very earliest period of Neolithic settlement. In addition, there are many surviving Neolithic burial sites that indicate the supreme importance these people attached to funerary ritual. They range from dolmens – two or three

● *The partly excavated burial mound at Knowth in the Boyne Valley*

● *Poulnabrone Dolmen, Co. Clare*

● *Proleek Dolmen, Ballymascanlon, Co. Louth.*

standing stones supporting a huge capstone – such as that at Poulnabrone in Co. Clare, to fully excavated passage graves, of which those in the Boyne Valley in Co. Meath are the most spectacular examples. The Boyne Valley is pre-Celtic Ireland's Valley of the Kings, a site of obvious religious significance both then and in later times. It is here that we find the three most famous Neolithic passage graves, those at Dowth, Knowth and – justly the most celebrated of all and one of the wonders of prehistoric Europe – at Newgrange.

Newgrange dates from about 2500 B.C. Its archaeological excavation in the 1960s was an outstanding achievement which uncovered this imposing and sophisticated structure for the first time in almost four millennia. The great circular cairn in which the passage grave itself is contained is over 100 metres in diameter. It was built with the greatest care and skill. For instance, the roofing stones were provided with shallow, concave channels to act as gutters, carrying rainwater towards the outside of the cairn and away from the burial chamber itself. Most famous of all is the carefully positioned light box at the entrance, aligned so that on the morning of the

winter solstice – and on that morning only – the rays of the rising sun penetrate the full distance of the passage into the burial chamber itself. The Neolithic people who built this extraordinary structure were not just simple farmers.

● *Drombeg Stone Circle, Co. Cork*

● *Decorative stonework at Newgrange*

They were skilled in construction techniques, in lapidary design and in astronomical observation.

Around 2000 B.C. the Bronze Age came to Ireland; many metal objects of great beauty still survive from this time. Irish Bronze Age metalwork was as fine as any in contemporary northern Europe, and was not confined simply to bronze. Gold was also popular and gold mining was an important economic activity. The Bronze Age was followed by the Iron Age, dating from about 250 B.C., and carried to the island primarily by the latest and most significant of its many waves of settlers: the Celts.

2. THE CELTS

We still think of Ireland, even today, as a Celtic country. Yet the Celts, when they first arrived from Europe around 250 B.C., were invaders just like the Mesolithic and Neolithic peoples before them.

The Celts came in waves, different tribal groups arriving at intervals over a period of centuries and settling in different parts of the country. The last of the major Celtic groups to invade Ireland were the *Gaeil*, who landed first in the south-east and gradually conquered the whole island, displacing the earlier Celtic settlers. By A.D. 400 the Gaelic conquest was total. It was this people, with their culture and language, who were to dominate Irish history for almost a thousand years. Their legacy is with us still.

The Gaelic world was soon divided between two powerful tribal coalitions: the *Eoghanacht* based in the southern half of the country and the *Connachta* in the north. Of the Connachta tribes, by far the most powerful and influential was the *Ui Neill*.

The Ui Neill were the ancestors of the modern O'Neills. By the end of the 6th century A.D., they dominated most of west Ulster and north Leinster. From their southern base at Tara, Co. Meath they claimed the high kingship of the entire island. This claim was never universally accepted, least of all by the Eoghanacht in the south, although they were not in a position to challenge the dominance of the Ui Neill. Beneath these two powerful provincial tribal groups, there was a network of about 150 *tuatha* or minor kingdoms, whose rulers were subordinate to regional overlords who in turn were subordinate to the provincial kings.

The Romans never thought Ireland worth conquering. The island missed out, therefore, on the great centralising and civilising effects of the Roman

● *A reconstructed Celtic crannog (lake dwelling) at Craggaunowen, Co. Clare*

Empire. However, there were compensations. Most notably, Ireland was a thoroughly Celtic – indeed, Gaelic – culture from the centre to the sea. It shared a common language, a common legal system and a common currency based on the value of cattle. This cultural unity coexisted with an ever-present militarism, as various tuatha fought each

● *The Rock of Cashel, Co. Tipperary, a Celtic*

● *A gold boat from the hoard of Celtic ornaments found at Broighter, Co. Derry*

● *A detail of the Tara Brooch*

stronghold where medieval buildings now stand

● *An Ogham stone. These stones, which bear an early form of Irish writing, are held to mark graves or boundaries.*

other back and forth for petty advantage in land, cattle and slaves. There was no strong political centre – the claims of the Ui Neill notwithstanding – which could hold the ring between the various warring factions. Gaelic Ireland was a culture without a state.

It was a highly stratified society, in which there were no less than 27 different classes of freemen. At the summit of the social scale, along with the petty kings, were the lawyers or *brehons*, the druids and the *fili* or poets. Economically, Gaelic Ireland was a pastoral, cattle-rearing society based on yeomen farmers who, although not of the aristocracy, were freemen. Most significantly, it was a completely rural society: the Gaels built no towns.

This fascinating, remote and undisturbed culture was not totally isolated, however. Irish raiding parties regularly attacked the British coast and for a time there were even Irish settlements in Wales. It was through this cross-channel activity that Gaelic society unwittingly opened the door for the first great intrusion into its secluded world: Christianity.

3. CHRISTIANITY

St Patrick, the national saint of Ireland and the most important of the country's Christian missionaries, was the son of a *decurio*, a civil servant in Roman Britain. He was abducted by Irish raiders as a young man and sold into slavery, probably near Slemish Mountain in Co. Antrim. After six years, he escaped and returned to Britain. He became a priest and later a bishop, returning to Ireland to spread the faith in response to a series of visions.

● *Slemish Mountain, Co. Antrim, where St Patrick was held in slavery*

● *A page from the Book of Kells*

Patrick was not the only Christian missionary in 5th-century Ireland. We know that in 431 Palladius was sent by Pope Celestine 'as the first bishop to the Irish who believe in Christ', which clearly suggests that Christians were already present on the island even at this early date. It seems most likely that Patrick was a true missionary, however, preaching the Gospel in pagan Ireland – probably in that part of central and eastern Ulster not yet dominated by the expanding kingdoms of the Ui Neill.

Significantly, Christianity was the state religion of the Roman Empire and so Roman civilisation at last reached Ireland. It did not overwhelm Gaelic Ireland, however. Rather, it took on protective local colouring, so that Irish Christianity soon diverged in a number of important respects from continental and Roman norms.

> *I saw in a dream a man called Victor who seemed to be from Ireland and had many letters. He gave me one and I read the opening words, "The Voice of the Irish". And as I read the beginning I seemed at that moment to hear the voice of those people ...*
> *They cried as with one voice: "We beg you, holy youth, come and walk once more among us."*
>
> *St Patrick* Confessions

The Irish Church, for example, was monastic rather than episcopal. There were no towns to act as foci for diocesan organisation, so monasteries assumed a great importance as centres of Christian learning, scholarship and discipline. But the effect of the new religion in the social sphere was more

● St Patrick's Bell Shrine

● Gallarus Oratory, Co. Kerry

monastic foundation at Clonmacnoise, Co. Offaly, was one of Europe's contemporary powerhouses of learning, justly earning early Christian Ireland the famous epithet of the 'island of saints and scholars'.

Irish Christianity also developed a hermitic tradition. There were many religious settlements in remote and inhospitable locations, none more so than on the Skellig rocks, off the Co. Kerry coast. Here hermits renounced all material comfort and lived lives of heroic self-sacrifice in atonement for the sins of the world.

Most of all, the early Irish Church was a missionary Church, reintroducing Christianity to the continent following the Roman imperial collapse. From Iona as far as Kiev, the Christian religion was carried back to a devastated and demoralised Europe. The early Irish missionary endeavour was a mighty outpouring of energy and dedication. Irish missionaries were everywhere, both within and without the boundaries of the old Roman Empire. They founded religious settlements all over northern, central and eastern Europe. The decline of Christianity had paralleled that of the Empire, so that even places like France and Italy needed to be re-evangelised. Germanic and Slav lands beyond the old imperial borders were brought within the Christian world for the first time. In all, it was a staggering achievement.

limited than in most other Christian countries. Divorce, for example, remained a secular matter and was still available under the Celts' Brehon Law, although anathema to orthodox Christianity.

There were many famous monasteries throughout Ireland, not least those at Glendalough, Co. Wicklow – founded by St Kevin – and at Kells, Co. Meath, whose chief treasure was the wonderful illuminated manuscript version of the four Gospels known appropriately as the Book of Kells. Irish monks were famed for their scholarship, especially in the Dark Ages following the collapse of the Roman Empire in the West. The

● The High Cross at Moone, Co. Kildare

4. THE VIKINGS

Viking raiders first appeared off the Irish coast in A.D. 795. Irish monasteries, with their precious ornaments and vessels, offered tempting targets to these intrepid pirates. Gradually, the scale of the raids increased and the Norsemen built coastal bases from which they forayed deep into the heart of the island. These were the first Irish towns. Dublin, Wexford, Waterford, Cork, Limerick: all owe their origins to the Vikings.

● *A reconstructed Viking longboat*

The Vikings burst in upon a stable, but also vulnerable, world. They were militarily more advanced than the Gaelic kings and their mastery of the longboat, as complete on Irish rivers as on the high seas, enabled them to move with terrifying speed. Monasteries were almost defenceless before them: the annals record a year-on-year catalogue of raids. It was in an attempt to survive these raids that the distinctive round towers were developed at monastic sites. Their doorways were well above head height and reached by ladders that could then be pulled up behind the fleeing monks.

The Vikings were ruthless plunderers but they were also traders. Their towns, especially Dublin, which they founded in 841, became centres of commerce, trading in particular with other Norse settlements in Britain such as York.

In time, the Gaelic kings began to grapple with the Vikings on more equal terms, and none more so than Mael Sechnaill, king of the southern Ui Neill at Tara. Yet he was not a national

● *Ardmore Church and Round Tower, Co. Waterford*

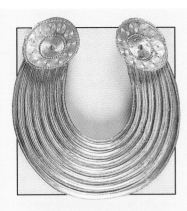

● *The Broighter Collar, typical of the precious objects sought by the Vikings*

leader, for there was no Gaelic nation in the modern, political sense. Indeed, the pattern soon emerged of a constantly shifting series of alliances between Gaels and Vikings, many of them directed against Mael Sechnaill, who was feared by other Gaelic kings as a potentially overwhelming threat.

The Vikings were merciless and efficient fighting men and the Gaels soon learned their ways. This introduced a seriously destabilising element into Ireland. Previously, the endemic wars between the tuatha had not disturbed the overall balance of Gaelic society or its political structures. Now, however, more effective and destructive military methods began to have that effect. As the Viking threat itself was gradually contained from about 900 onward, Gaelic warlords could use the lessons they had learned from the Norsemen to shatter the equilibrium of the old order.

The most spectacular winner in this game was a small tuath from east Co. Clare called *Dal Chais*. As the traditional Eoghanacht power in Munster declined, the kings of Dal Chais spread out from their ancestral heartland into Eoghanacht territory, while also reducing the Norse settlement of Limerick.

In 976, Brian Boru became king of Dal Chais. Two years later, he broke Eoghanacht power forever at the battle of Belach Lechtna in Co. Cork and became king of Munster. He then waged war against the southern Ui Neill, and by 1005 had done what no one had thought possible – gained effective control of the whole island by securing the submission of all the Ui Neill, both the northern and southern branches. Here was a high king in the literal sense of the term.

Brian was a revolutionary but his revolution did not last. The Leinstermen and their Norse allies revolted against him and engaged him in battle at Clontarf, near Dublin, in April 1014. Brian's army routed their enemy but at a price, for the high king himself was killed. With him died the possibility of a united Gaelic kingdom.

● *The Round Tower at Glendalough, Co. Wicklow*

5. THE ANGLO-NORMANS

The battle at Clontarf was not a contest between Irish defenders and Viking intruders. It was part of the endless series of conflicts between Irish warlords, in which the Norsemen of Dublin – plus some Viking mercenaries specially shipped in from the Isle of Man – were recruited on the side of the Leinstermen. The Munstermen's victory was a pyrrhic one, for it both robbed them of their king and so weakened

● *Carrickfergus Castle, Co. Antrim*

● *Dunguaire Castle, near Kinvara, Co. Galway, a fine medieval tower house*

them that they could no longer aspire to that all-Ireland sovereignty which had been the essence of Brian Boru's claim to the high kingship. There was to be no strong political centre in Gaelic Ireland. Instead, the old pattern resumed. The O'Briens (as the Dal Chais successors of Brian Boru now called themselves) fought for supremacy with the Ui Neill,

although by the middle of the 12th century both groups had been eclipsed by the rising power of the O'Conors of Connacht. Their claim to the high kingship, however, was little better than nominal, as events were soon to prove.

Everything was turned upside down by the arrival of the Anglo-Normans in 1169. The Normans were descendants of Viking marauders who had settled in Normandy; in 1066 they had conquered England and gradually extended their supremacy over most of Britain. They were but one element of a vast imperial enterprise which carried the culture of Charlemagne's successors from its heartland between the Loire and the

---

The Normans first landed at Baginbun beach, in south Co. Wexford. The chronicler Richard Stanihurst, writing over four centuries later, summed up their arrival in a couplet:
At the creek of Baginbun Ireland was lost and won

Rhine to places as far flung as Riga, Sicily – and Ireland. It was to the Norman king, Henry II, that Diarmuid MacMurrough, the deposed king of Leinster, turned for help in an attempt to recover his kingdom.

MacMurrough had first become king of Leinster around 1126. In 1152 he abducted the wife of a neighbouring king, O'Rourke of Breffni (roughly modern Co. Cavan), and sparked the series of events that finally led to his defeat and his mission to Henry II.

Henry was too busy to bother about the squabbles of Irish sub-kings but the internal chaos of Ireland made it promising territory for further Norman expansion. Henry therefore gave

● *Clonfert Cathedral, Co. Galway*

based on the alien concept of primogeniture, highly sophisticated construction techniques and an irresistible military expertise. The Gaels were swept aside, as often by honeyed words as by the sword, for the Normans had no intention of honouring promises to uphold traditional Gaelic rights and liberties. They conquered vast tracts of land and established their leading men as lords, in defiance of Gaelic laws and customs which they considered simply barbarous. They built magnificent military structures like King John's Castle in Limerick and Carrickfergus Castle in Co. Antrim, and by 1250 had effectively accomplished that which the Vikings had never even attempted: the conquest and ownership of more than three-quarters of the island of Ireland – including most of the best land.

● *Art MacMurrough Kavanagh attacking the king's troops under the command of the Earl of Gloucester, in the Wicklow hills.*

Diarmuid permission to drum up support among the restless and aggressive Norman lords of the Welsh marches.

Diarmuid's principal recruit was Richard de Clare, better known as Strongbow, under whose leadership the Norman invasion took place. The vastly superior military skills of the Normans swept aside initial opposition and soon they had possession of the east coast towns, most significantly Dublin. In 1171, Henry II came over and received the submission not only of the new Norman colonists but of most Gaelic kings as well. Thus began the long and fateful involvement of the English crown in Ireland.

The Normans might as well have come from another world. They brought European feudalism, a legal system

● *The Abbey of Holy Cross, on the River Suir in Co. Tipperary, founded in 1180*

6. MEDIEVAL IRELAND

To the victor the spoils. Norman troops conquered the land, Norman lawyers drew up the deeds of ownership and Norman builders built the tower houses and castles that secured what had been won.

In two generations, vast tracts of land had passed out of Gaelic control, leaving only scattered pockets, mainly in the west. The largest such pocket was in western Ulster, where the modern counties of Donegal and Tyrone remained in the hands of the O'Donnells and the O'Neills (the successors of the northern Ui Neill). The rest of the country comprised first an area around Dublin known as the Pale, which was administered directly by the Crown, and secondly the great liberties of the Norman feudal magnates who, although ultimately loyal to the Crown, resented any encroachment on their territories. Liberties were autonomous territories in which the magnates controlled the administration of justice, the collection of revenue and the keeping of the peace. The king's writ was as unwelcome to them as the threat of a Gaelic resurgence.

That resurgence came at the start of the 14th century. Gaelic chieftains pressed alike on the Pale and on the semi-independent Norman liberties. The Gaels had two great advantages: first, force of numbers, for the colonists

● *Moyne Friary cloisters, Co. Mayo*

● *Athenry Castle, Co. Galway*

were thin on the ground; second, their laws of succession which decreed that a king could be succeeded by any of his male relatives who shared a common great-grandfather. This may have been responsible for many of the endemic quarrels in Gaelic society, but now it

● *A selection of medieval artefacts from Cork city*

● *Jerpoint Abbey, Co. Kilkenny*

came to the rescue because of the wide range of people always available to succeed a fallen king. The Normans could defeat Gaelic kings; Gaelic kingdoms were a bit more durable. In addition, the Gaels learned Norman ways as they had once learned Norse ones. They became more sophisticated in military affairs and began importing mercenaries from Scotland.

By the middle of the 14th century, all

● *The Butler tomb, St Canice's Cathedral, Kilkenny*

● *Medieval baptismal font, St Mary's Church, Youghal, Co. Cork*

of Connacht except for the town of Galway had been recovered and all of Ulster except for Carrickfergus. The Pale had shrunk. Only the great Norman magnates of the south and east – the FitzGeralds of Kildare and Desmond and the Butlers of Ormond – were proof against the Gaelic resurgence, and many of these were themselves relatively 'Gaelicised' through inter-marriage and the adoption of the Irish language. This was especially true of the FitzGeralds of Desmond.

This Gaelic cultural infiltration of the Norman colony led to the passing of the Statutes of Kilkenny (1366), an attempt to forbid by legislation the wearing of Gaelic dress, the speaking of Irish or the adoption of various other undesirable Gaelic attributes by the Anglo-Normans. The statutes were largely ignored.

So pressing had the Gaelic resurgence become by the end of the century that King Richard II himself came over twice, principally to defeat the Gaelic chieftain Art MacMurrough Kavanagh who had for years been attacking the southern borders of the Pale. This the king failed to do on both occasions, underlining the weakness of royal power in Ireland.

That weakness further accelerated the independence of the Norman magnates who, in the absence of effective royal power, were happy to look after themselves. The Earldom of Desmond in West Munster was for all practical purposes an independent state in the first half of the 15th century. But the greatest of the magnate families was the other branch of the FitzGeralds, based in Kildare, which was set to dominate Ireland for two generations.

7. GERALDINE IRELAND

In the long series of English dynastic struggles known as the Wars of the Roses, both sides – the houses of York and Lancaster – were glad of support from the great Anglo-Norman families. Both branches of the FitzGeralds, Desmond and Kildare, were Yorkists. The Butlers of Ormond were Lancastrians. By 1461, the Yorkists had triumphed in the person of King Edward IV. He first appointed the Earl of Desmond as chief governor of Ireland, but when the earl proved to be too Gaelicised in his ways, the king had him summarily beheaded. The Butlers, as Lancastrian supporters, were obvious non-starters for governorship. That left the house of Kildare. It acquired the chief governorship in 1470, lost it briefly, then was threatened with having to share it with an Englishman. All these expedients failed and by 1478, Gearoid Mor FitzGerald, 8th Earl of Kildare, was chief governor of Ireland. He might more properly have been called king of Ireland, so total was his authority.

The FitzGeralds of Kildare were enormously rich and well connected, related by birth and marriage to a huge network of Anglo-Norman and Gaelic families alike. The rule of Gearoid Mor

● Elizabeth FitzGerald, known as the 'Fair Geraldine', was the daughter of Garret Og FitzgGerald, 9th Earl of Kildare, and the sister of Silken Thomas.

– the Great Earl – was the high-water mark of Anglo-Norman magnate power in Ireland. The central administration, far away over the water in London, had not the resources or the military means or the will to enforce direct rule.

What was unusual about the Great Earl was not his position but the all-embracing extent of his power. He was ruthless in his determination to ensure the undiluted supremacy of the house of Kildare and in this he was completely successful. Even the return of the Lancastrians in 1485 in the shape of Henry Tudor, who ascended the English throne as Henry VII, failed to shake the Great Earl's position. The king did manage to dismiss Kildare briefly in the 1490s, replacing him with an Englishman, Sir Edward Poynings, the author of the celebrated Poynings' Law of 1494 which made acts of the Irish parliament subject to English approval, a provision which was less important at the time than it was to become later.

● The interior of Bunratty Castle, Co. Clare. Originally medieval, it has been restored in modern times.

Yet the king, a man inclined towards economy, had no intention of maintaining Poynings and an army in Ireland indefinitely. In 1496, he was recalled, the Great Earl was restored and held his position till his death in 1513. He was succeeded by his son Gearoid Og, the 9th earl who, like his father, was removed briefly in the early 1520s only to be quickly reinstated. He continued in office until 1534, when there occurred one of the seismic shifts in the history of Ireland.

The Kildare ascendancy had meant that Ireland could be governed in the king's name without the king having to pay for it. The Earls of Kildare controlled the country through their own armies or those of their family allies; they received

● *King Henry VII*

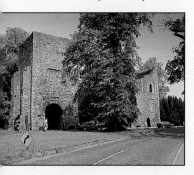

● *The 13th-century gatehouse of Maynooth Castle, Co. Kildare, seat of the Earls of Kildare*

● *The De Burgho-O'Malley Chalice*

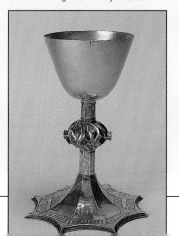

● *Aughnanure Castle, near Oughterard, Co. Galway, a well-preserved 15th-century tower house*

the revenues from taxation; they controlled patronage and jobs. It is interesting, however, that they never took the fateful step of attempting to proclaim themselves kings of Ireland. For all their awesome power, the earls answered to England in the end. And by the early 16th century, England was locked in the grip of a religious and constitutional revolution that would sweep their world away.

8. TUDOR IRELAND

The Tudor revolution in England began as a desperate search for a means to allow King Henry VIII to divorce his wife. It ended with the creation of a new kind of European state. To effect the divorce, the king renounced the spiritual authority of the pope and himself became head of the Church of England. In addition, he was determined to centralise power and to reduce the influence of provincial magnates. This had obvious implications for Ireland. The English of

● *Rothe House in Kilkenny city, a particularly good example of a late medieval merchant's town-house*

● *Rothe House courtyard*

the Pale were great enthusiasts for the new regime. They plotted against the Earl of Kildare, who was duly summoned to London. He left his son Lord Offaly – better known to history as Silken Thomas – in charge with instructions to make a show of force if he himself was dismissed from office. Not only was Kildare dismissed but he was clapped in the Tower of London, from where premature rumours of his death reached Ireland. Silken Thomas's show of force – originally designed to prove yet again that only the Kildare family faction could rule Ireland and that the cost of suppressing them would be prohibitive – now turned into outright rebellion. This was quickly and decisively crushed by an English army. In 1536, Kildare died in the Tower; in 1537, Silken Thomas was executed. Within three years, the power of the FitzGeralds had been broken utterly. This was a very new way of dealing with Ireland.

Just as he had snuffed out Welsh

● *Pope Pius V, who excommunicated Queen Elizabeth I and released her Catholic subjects from obedience to her*

● *Sir John Perrott, President of Munster in the 1570s and Lord Deputy of Ireland in the 1580s*

● *Dating from 1569, the manor house of 'Black Tom' Butler, 10th Earl of Ormond, stands outside Carrick-on-Suir, Co. Tipperary. It is one of the first examples in Ireland of an unfortified manor house. Note the ruins of the fortified Norman tower house in the background.*

independence and reduced the power of the magnates in the north of England, Henry was determined that his writ would run throughout his realm, administered not by over-mighty subjects but by a new, loyal English bureaucracy, judiciary and clergy. The king gained control of the Irish Church by the same means he had used in England. He dissolved the monasteries and remitted their revenues to the state. He also made himself formally king of Ireland in 1541: his predecessors had contented themselves with the title Lord of Ireland. He obliged the Gaelic chieftains to acknowledge his sovereign power by surrendering their lands to him, whereupon he granted them back – but under English legal title. What Henry VIII did not do was introduce British colonists to Ireland.

These were not long in coming after his death, however. His daughter Mary encouraged colonisation – plantation – in the midlands in the 1550s but the religious reformation awaited the accession of her sister, Queen Elizabeth, in 1558. Henry VIII's revolution in Church and State had created a fertile ground for the spread of Reformation ideas in England, and although he himself never adopted the new faith, Elizabeth did. She was to reign for 45 years.

The first thirty-odd years of that reign brought a constant push of new English settlers into Gaelic and Anglo-Norman areas. East Ulster was planted in the 1560s and 1570s. The earldom of Desmond, which was wedded alike to the old religion and the old political ways, was goaded into rebellion and defeated with great savagery. Thus the way was open for the plantation of English settlers in Munster.

The queen, like her grandfather Henry VII, was parsimonious and baulked at the cost of a thoroughgoing conquest of Ireland. Yet that was the direction in which events were pushing her. The new English state – now a growing European power nervous of the unconquered island at its back door – was about to lock horns in a deadly tussle with Gaelic Ireland.

9. THE NINE YEARS' WAR

From the 1540s on, there had been tension between the new English state and the Gaelic world. The 'middle nation' of the Anglo-Normans – or the Old English as they were known from then on, to distinguish them from the Reformation New English – had been neutralised politically by the destruction first of the Kildare FitzGeralds and then of their Desmond cousins. More and more, the steady incursions of the New English pressed upon Gaelic territory.

Most of all, this was true of Ulster. It was here that the world of the Gaelic Irish, over a thousand years old, made

● *Charles Blount, Lord Mountjoy, victor at the Battle of Kinsale*

Whatever man is not on our side and will not spend himself in the interests of justice, we take him to be a man against us. Therefore, wherever you do good for yourself do us ill to the best of your ability, and we will do you ill to the best of ours, with God's will.

Hugh O'Neill, from a letter to an enemy, translated from Irish

● *English troops ride out of Dublin Castle in the 1580s. Note the heads of rebels on spikes over the main gate.*

what was effectively its last stand. Its leader was Hugh O'Neill, who was head of the historic O'Neill clan and also feudal lord of Tyrone under English law. Such dual arrangements were quite common at the margins of 16th-century states. Opposing him was Sir Henry Bagenal, a member of the leading New English family in South Ulster. English monarchs had traditionally ruled through alliances with people like O'Neill. Now that was all to end. O'Neill was no longer going to have the freedom to administer Ulster according to traditional Gaelic law and custom in return for keeping the peace. The queen's law would henceforth be the

● *Above left: Robert Devereux, Earl of Essex, a military failure in Ireland*
● *Above right: Hugh O'Neill*

only law in any part of her realm and Sir Henry Bagenal was the man to bring it to Ulster.

That, at least, was what Sir Henry Bagenal thought. Unfortunately for him, he was up against an exceptionally gifted man. Hugh O'Neill was cunning, powerful, ruthless and intelligent. Moreover, he was skilled at making alliances with subordinate Gaelic chieftains, like the dashing Red Hugh O'Donnell of Donegal, and then holding them to their bargains.

For years, there had been pressure on south-west Ulster from the New English of Connacht. Finally, in 1594, they captured Enniskillen Castle, a vital point of entry to the O'Neill heartland. O'Neill's supreme ability as a deal-maker, his capacity to be all things to all men, to make alliances and bargains with Gaels, Old English, New English and government alike was no use to him now. This was a challenge that had to be met head on. By 1595 he was in open rebellion.

He was well equipped for a defensive war. He was on home ground, and Ulster was a natural fortress protected by a series of low hills and lakes. There

were only four or five passes through which an army could be marched into the O'Neill heartland. Furthermore, Ulster was badly mapped, another problem for invading troops. O'Neill's two triumphs over Bagenal, at Clontibret and the Yellow Ford, were both defensive ambush battles of the

● *Donegal Castle, the stronghold of Red Hugh O'Donnell*

traditional Gaelic kind. What O'Neill was neither equipped for nor skilled at was offensive, regular warfare. For this he needed the sort of allies that were not available in Ireland. So he made a fateful decision, and sent an emissary to England's mortal enemy, Spain.

Thus was Ireland first drawn into the European wars of religion. King Philip III of Spain sent an army to Ireland, which landed at Kinsale, Co. Cork – at the far end of the island from O'Neill's homeland – in 1601. O'Neill marched south to join them. In the battle at Kinsale which followed, the English, under the command of Lord Mountjoy, routed the Hiberno-Spanish forces. It was, for all practical purposes, the end of Gaelic Ireland.

10. THE PLANTATION OF ULSTER

The defeat at Kinsale was followed by some further sporadic resistance, but by 1603 it was all over. Hugh O'Neill surrendered to Lord Mountjoy and submitted to royal authority. Ulster was shired, English law introduced into what was hitherto the most Gaelic part of the island and the whole basis of O'Neill's traditional power was subverted. Within four years, he had had enough. With the O'Donnells of Donegal and their various relatives and retainers, he took ship at Lough Swilly in September 1607, bound for the continent. None of them returned.

This was the 'Flight of the Earls'. It left Ulster in the hands of an unyielding and unscrupulous Dublin administration set upon the final destruction of what they saw as Gaelic barbarism and its replacement with English civility. They lost no time in declaring all the O'Neill and O'Donnell lands forfeit to the crown. The next move was to draw up a comprehensive scheme for the wholesale plantation of the now vacant land with reliable, loyal English and Scots Protestants.

Over two million acres of fertile land in West Ulster were settled in this way. The natives were left with an area less than half that size, mainly comprising poor upland country. Traditionally, East

● *Modern Derry. The 17th-century walls are still in existence.*

Ulster had close ties to Scotland and private plantation schemes went ahead there, achieving substantially the same effect as the government plantation in the west. Other parts of Ireland were also planted in the early 17th century, but none so thoroughly or so successfully as Ulster. Only here was there established a substantial and coherent Protestant population. The rest of the island remained overwhelmingly Catholic.

The English and Scots planters transformed Ulster. They built towns, developed commerce, vastly improved agricultural techniques, cleared thousands of acres of woodland, and introduced modern architectural methods. They were a radical, modernising force suddenly thrust into an archaic world. Gaelic society had been remote and, like many remote parts of Europe, it had valued its traditional independence from central authority. In effect, the Nine Years' War had been fought to protect these regional liberties. But the war had been lost, and the losers were replaced by a very different kind of people.

The Ulster Protestants were self-conscious agents of modernisation. They were the product of a society

● *Ballygally Castle, Co. Antrim, a fine early plantation house dating from 1625*

which was technically much more advanced than the Gaelic world. Most of all, they were politically different. They were dutiful subjects of a modernised, Protestant kingdom – the most highly developed nation state in Europe at the time. In place of the old Gaelic particularism, with its decentralised, local loyalties, they brought a sense of citizenship. Their loyalty was to the state, to the king at its centre and to the king's law which was the same for them as for people in London or Bristol.

● *Above: the lush countryside of the Ards Peninsula, first planted by English settlers in the 1560s*

● *The cloth workers' building ,Coleraine, Co. Derry, standing across the River Bann from the walled plantation town*

The Plantation of Ulster sowed the seeds of the modern troubles in Northern Ireland by introducing colonial settlers whose sense of superiority to the displaced natives meant that the two groups could not assimilate. The natives, meanwhile, were humbled but not destroyed. They answered the superiority of their conquerors with enmity and resentment. The Ulster Protestants soon found themselves in a state of more or less perpetual mental siege, forever fearing a Catholic resurgence. It was a process not unique to Ireland. All over contemporary Europe, and especially in German borderlands in Poland and Bohemia, a similar pattern of colonial settlement was in train. Advanced cultures tend to prey upon less developed ones.

● *John Knox, the Scottish Calvinist reformer, whose influence was felt among the Presbyterian settlers in Ulster*

11. EARLY STUART IRELAND

When Queen Elizabeth died childless in 1603, the throne passed to her cousin James VI of Scotland who thus became James I of England. He was succeeded by his son Charles I, who reigned from 1625 until his execution in 1649.

● *James I of England before he ascended the English throne. At this point he was King James VI of Scotland.*

The union of crowns did not mean a union of religion, for the English Reformation had resulted in a Church of England which, while Protestant, was generally closer to Lutheranism than to Calvinism. On the other hand, Scotland was solidly Calvinist. In Ireland, the New English were Protestants to a man, with a strong Calvinist element among them. (The Scots planters in Ulster were, of course, Calvinist through and through.) The Old English remained Catholic for the most part, one of the few influential groups in the British Isles among whom the Counter-Reformation was a resounding success. The Gaels, as might be expected, were never seduced by the charms of the Reformation.

● *Top: King Charles I*
● *Above: Thomas Wentworth, Earl of Strafford, ruler of Ireland in the 1630s*

In the first half of the 17th century, therefore, the great majority of Irish land outside Ulster still lay in Catholic hands. Moreover, even in Ulster itself there was a large population of Catholic tenants and labourers. True, Protestant adventurers like Richard Boyle, the Great Earl of Cork, acquired vast estates in Munster by fair means and foul, but they remained islands of the Reformation in an ocean of Catholicism.

Nevertheless, the New English Protestants controlled the Dublin administration, the Irish parliament and the law: in short, the effective engines of political power. In religion, they had a pronounced Calvinist streak, which did not always commend them to the Stuarts. Scots background or no, both James I and Charles I were moderate Anglicans and were reasonably indulgent towards Irish Catholic landowners. This indulgence arose less from a spirit of innate toleration than from a constant need for cash, not least to pay for the defence of Ireland against possible invasion by Spain. It made sense not to alienate the Old English, in particular, for they were the richest single group in Ireland and therefore the most promising source of revenue.

In 1628, the Old English extracted from Charles I a series of promises and undertakings known as the Graces, in which they pledged a total of £120,000 to the king over two years. In return, he undertook to confirm their land titles and to relieve New English pressure upon them. The king, however, took the cash but did not keep his side of the bargain for more than a few years, until the threat of war and invasion had passed. All the time, he was under pressure from the English Calvinists who were a powerful interest in England and who fully supported the claims of their New English friends in Ireland.

In 1633, the king sent a new governor to Ireland. Thomas Wentworth, later Earl of Strafford, was an authoritarian. At first, both New and Old English fancied that they had a friend. Both soon found an enemy. Wentworth disliked the New English because of their Calvinism; he, like the king, was an episcopalian. He disliked the Old English because of their stubborn Catholicism and their refusal, as an influential group, to conform to the state religion. Consequently, he managed to antagonise people on every side, not least by trying to increase greatly the tax revenue from Ireland. No group was spared his exactions. In the end, however, his rule was a failure: he was recalled and lost his life in the great political storm that was gathering over both islands.

● *St Patrick's Purgatory at Lough Derg, Co. Donegal. In 1632 it was destroyed on the orders of the Anglican Bishop of Clogher in accordance with instructions from the government.*

● *Irish soldiers in the service of King Gustavus Adolphus of Sweden, 1631. The mercenaries are in the city of Stettin on the Baltic.*

12. CATASTROPHE

The reason the king needed to soak Ireland for tax revenues was simple. Charles I wanted to be a king along the emerging French or Spanish lines, that is, an absolute monarch answerable only to God. Therefore, he tried to rule without parliament. From 1629 to 1640, he succeeded. But it was only by grant of parliament that the king could raise revenue legally. As a result, for most of those eleven years he was strapped for cash and looked to Wentworth to squeeze it out of the Irish.

At one Mr Atkins house 7 Papistes brake in & beate out his braines, then riped upe his Wife with childe after they had rauished her & Nero like vewed natures bed of conception then tooke they the Childe and sacrificed it in the fire

C

● *The Protestant memory of the horrors of the Rebellion of 1641 was nurtured by illustrations such as this.*

The king desired uniform Anglicanism throughout his realm, and this drove the Scots Calvinists to rebellion. It was the need to finance a war against them that caused him at last to recall parliament in 1640. But his relations with the parliamentary leaders, most of them Calvinists themselves, were so poor that by 1642 the two sides had taken up arms against each other in the English Civil War.

By then, however, Ireland was alight. In October 1641, the Catholic landowners of Ulster took advantage of all this turmoil and revolted against the Dublin administration. They hoped to effect at least a partial undoing of the Plantation of Ulster. They were quickly joined by a coalition of Catholic landowners, both Old English and Gaelic, from Leinster and Munster, and in 1642 these groups formed a quasi-parliamentary assembly known as the Confederation of Kilkenny.

In the meantime, events in Ulster had taken an ugly turn. The rebellion quickly turned into a vicious assault upon the settler population by embittered and dispossessed natives. There were massacres and atrocities. Protestant churches were desecrated; corpses were exhumed and flung about; and many thousands of Protestants of all ages were butchered. The numbers killed were probably exaggerated afterwards but 1641 is, nevertheless, a date burned indelibly into the Ulster Protestant consciousness.

The main rebellion failed in its aim of capturing Dublin Castle. The Confederation of Kilkenny had, however, raised an army under the command of Owen Roe O'Neill, a nephew of the great Hugh O'Neill and himself a Spanish army veteran. Meanwhile, the Ulster Protestants, now hysterical with fear, felt themselves delivered from immediate danger by the arrival of an army of Scots

● *The cathedral on the Rock of Cashel which was captured and burned by Lord Inchiquin in 1647*

● James Butler, first Duke of Ormond, leader of the Royalist forces in Ireland during the 1640s and Lord Lieutenant of Ireland at the Restoration

● A stylised portrait of Owen Roe O'Neill, military leader of the Gaelic Irish during the 1640s

Covenanters under the command of General George Munro.

There were now three main groups in Ireland. First, the Ulster Protestants, who were determined to resist any further depredations against them. Second, there was the royal administration in Dublin, now in the hands of James Butler, Earl (later Duke) of Ormond, a member of one of the great Old English houses but a Protestant none the less. The third group, the Confederates, were divided between the Gaelic element which, egged on by Owen Roe O'Neill and the

● Archbishop Rinuccini, papal delegate to the Confederation of Kilkenny

papal nuncio Archbishop Rinuccini, wanted to press Catholic claims to the utmost, and the more cautious Old English.

In military terms, no group was strong enough to overwhelm the rest. O'Neill defeated Munro in the major battle of the war at Benburb in 1646 but did not have the means to follow up his success and launch his army against Ulster. The resulting stalemate meant that whoever won the English Civil War would be able to crack the whip in Ireland. The climax came with stunning clarity in 1649 when the parliamentary victory was followed by the execution of the king. A parliamentary army was soon sailing for Ireland to settle matters there. Its leader was Oliver Cromwell.

13. CROMWELL

Cromwell 'like a lightning passed through the land'. The leader of the victorious parliamentary forces in England was a soldier and organiser of genius. He had at his disposal perhaps the finest fighting force in contemporary Europe, his New Model Army. They were tough, battle hardened and disciplined. They were also fired with a sense of mission, for they were Puritans – as English Calvinists now called themselves – and saw themselves as avengers, come to settle the account with those responsible for the Ulster massacres of 1641.

Within two months, Cromwell had the eastern half of the island substantially under his control. In

● Oliver Cromwell

● The ruins of Cromwell's Bridge, near Glengarriff, Co. Cork. It is said to have been built, by order of Cromwell, at an hour's notice.

This is a righteous judgment of God upon those barbarous wretches, who have imbrued their hands in so much innocent blood.

Cromwell, after the massacre of an estimated 2000 soldiers and clergy following the storming of Drogheda

September, he took Drogheda and butchered the entire garrison in an act of vengeance that shocked even a Europe familiar with the horrors of the Thirty Years' War. In October, the same treatment was meted out to Wexford. He then moved into Munster, meeting little resistance from towns that had no desire to suffer the fate of Drogheda and Wexford. By the time he returned to England, all that was left was a mopping-up operation, which in the end took longer than it should. Still, by 1652, the Cromwellians had even taken the remote island of Inishbofin, off the coast of Co. Galway. They were masters of all Ireland.

Cromwell now determined upon a wholesale revolution in Ireland unlike anything seen before. He dispossessed every Catholic landowner in the country, on the grounds that all Catholics had been complicit in the 1641 massacres. Fine distinctions between Gaelic landowners and the Old English did not trouble him: he was the first figure in Irish history to act upon the assumption that Catholics were an undifferentiated, homogeneous group and should be treated accordingly.

Eleven million acres of land were confiscated. On them were settled a

Withdraw your scouring stick.

● *A musketeer of Cromwell's New Model Army*

● *Sir William Petty, the brilliant surveyor who was responsible for the Down Survey of the 1650s*

mixture of adventurers and soldiers, the former having been investors whose money had supported the parliamentary armies and who were now due their dividend. By the mid 1650s, not a single Catholic landowner remained in possession east of the River Shannon, an area where twenty years before over 80 per cent of land had been in Catholic hands. Most of Connacht west of the Shannon – some of the poorest land in the country – was kept as a reservation for those displaced Catholics who had neither escaped to the continent nor been shipped off to the West Indies as indentured servants, a polite name for slaves. The new Cromwellian *herrenvolk* now in control of the land of Ireland would, as their manners gradually grew less coarse, mutate into what became known as the Protestant Ascendancy.

In technical terms, the Cromwellian plantation was a remarkable achievement. It was made possible by the brilliance of Sir William Petty, the Surveyor-General of Ireland, whose survey of the whole country – known as the Down Survey – was the most accurate mapping of the island ever attempted up to that time.

The Cromwellian plantation set the pattern for Irish land ownership until the early 20th century. Cromwellian politics proved less durable. England wearied of Puritan rule; Cromwell himself died in 1658; two years later Charles II was bid home from his travels to take his place upon his father's throne. The Stuarts were back.

● *Inishbofin, off the coast of Co. Galway, was the last part of Irish territory captured by Cromwellian forces.*

14. RESTORATION IRELAND

The new king was cynical, worldly and genial. Most of all, he was of a mind to keep his head on his shoulders and his throne beneath him, unlike his father. That meant not offending powerful interest groups. Accordingly, he had long since agreed with the Scots that their Presbyterian Church organisation was acceptable to him, thus abandoning the attempt to enforce episcopalian uniformity throughout his realm, the lost cause which had started Charles I on his slide to disaster.

As with Scotland, so with Ireland. Charles may not have found the new Cromwellian landlord class very congenial, but there was no possibility of his ever being able substantially to dispossess them or to reverse the land settlement generally. This was a sore

● King Charles II

● Robert Boyle, son of the great Earl of Cork and a famous chemist. He studied the behaviour of gases, formulated Boyle's law and helped to dissociate chemistry from alchemy.

● The king returns to England. Charles II lands at Dover and accepts the homage of his subjects.

disappointment to many people, most of all to those Old English who had stood by him and who were now to be denied their reward. Of course, there were some who simply could not be ignored. Most obviously, James Butler was restored to his historic patrimony and created 1st Duke of Ormond. He was to dominate Irish government for most of Charles's reign.

● Above left: St Oliver Plunkett
● Above right: Richard Talbot, Duke of Tyrconnell, the leader of the Old English nobility who prospered under James II

To the extent that he had any strong religious feelings, Charles II was a moderate Anglican and, for the most part, he left the Catholics of Ireland in peace. Only the hysteria following the so-called 'Popish Plot' in England brought a brief persecution – although this was enough, in 1681, to see the judicial murder of St Oliver Plunkett, the archbishop of Armagh and a member of one of oldest Old English families of the Pale.

● King Charles' fort at Kinsale, Co. Cork, the best surviving example of a 17th-century coastal fortress in Ireland

The king's brother, however, was a Roman Catholic. The Duke of York was both intelligent and unpleasant. Even worse, he had some of his father's hankering for absolutism, now at its continental zenith at the court of Louis XIV in France. In 1685, Charles died without an heir and the Duke of York succeeded him as King James II. For Irish Catholics, and for the Old English in particular, it must have seemed like a moment of deliverance. Not since Queen Mary had died in 1558 had one of their co-religionists been on the throne. James was, of course, an object of intense suspicion in England, by now a thoroughly Protestant country – to say nothing of Presbyterian Scotland. But in Ireland, all the hopes of the Old English were fulfilled. One of their leading men, Richard Talbot, was appointed Duke of Tyrconnell and given charge of the army with instructions to strengthen it. He was also given the position of Lord-in-General and quickly moved to replace Protestants with Old English Catholics in the Irish administration. Most of all, he held out every hope of restoring Catholics to their lost lands.

In England, Tyrconnell's Irish army was viewed with the gravest suspicion as a potential means of establishing royal absolutism. This fear turned to conspiracy when the queen produced a male heir, thus securing the Catholic succession. A *coup d'état* in the Protestant interest brought the Dutchman William of Orange, husband of James II's daughter Mary, to the English throne, an event later dignified as the Glorious Revolution. James fled to Ireland, his natural power base, and summoned the so-called 'patriot parliament' which was, in fact, an assembly of the Catholic Old English. It was their swan song, for they were about to disappear from history forever.

15. THE WILLIAMITE WAR

The Glorious Revolution was welcomed in Protestant Ulster and among the Cromwellian settlers in Leinster and Munster. They watched with horror as the patriot parliament disendowed the Church of Ireland and began the process of undoing the land settlement. At the same time, James's forces gathered themselves and moved north into Ulster. Soon the whole province lay at their mercy except for the walled plantation towns of Derry and Enniskillen.

On 18 April 1689, King James II presented himself before the walls of Derry. He was fired on by the

Our necessity of eating the composition of tallow and starch did not only nourish and support us, but was an infallible cure for the looseness.

George Walker, A True History of the Siege of Londonderry

Protestants gathered within, their numbers already swollen by refugees from the countryside. The gates were slammed against the Jacobite army and the siege of Derry was on. It seemed a hopeless undertaking. The Jacobites had effectively taken Ulster: a month earlier, at Dromore, Co. Down, on the far side of the province, they had defeated a Protestant army with ease. Now this tiny walled town, bursting with civilians, children and old people as well as troops, was supposed to hold out against a conquering army.

But they did. Conditions within the walls were vile (they were, for example, reduced to eating vermin) but they resisted for 105 days. In the meantime a Williamite army had landed at Larne, Co. Antrim, and eventually Williamite ships broke the Jacobite boom across the River Foyle and allowed supplies into the starving town.

● *King James II*

● *The Battle of the Boyne, 1690*

● *The Treaty Stone, Limerick, on which the Treaty of Limerick was supposedly signed. King John's Castle lies behind.*

By now, this war had become a minor sideshow in the greater European conflict known as the War of the League of Augsburg. The contending forces were the French and a coalition of interests put together by William of Orange. King Louis XIV of France was quite happy to see Anglo-Dutch forces tied up in Ireland, far from the main action of the war, and so the Jacobites were reinforced with French troops. After the Jacobite failure before Derry, the initiative began to slip slowly out of their hands, although they still controlled most of Ireland outside Ulster. In June 1690 William of Orange landed at Carrickfergus, Co. Antrim, and made his way south. On 1 July, he met James at the Battle of the Boyne and defeated him in the largest, most fabled and arguably most important battle in Irish history. James fled to Dublin and later sailed for France, where he lived out the remaining ten years of his life.

William, too, found little to detain him further in Ireland. He also departed, leaving the conduct of the war in the hands of his capable general, Ginkel. The Williamite progress was steady, although they met heavy resistance at Limerick, which they were forced to besiege. The defenders of Limerick were led by the Frenchman Boisileau but it was his Old English second-in-command, Patrick Sarsfield, who most distinguished himself.

The first siege of Limerick was raised but in July 1691 there came the battle that finally broke the back of the Jacobite cause and with it the remaining Old English influence in the history of Ireland. Ginkel routed the Jacobites under the incompetent Frenchman St Ruth at Aughrim, Co. Galway. (The French had no intention of sending one of their better generals to such an unimportant theatre of the war.) The Jacobite cavalry, mostly Old English, retreated in good order; the Gaelic infantry was slaughtered.

● *King William III, Prince of Orange*

The Jacobites retreated to Limerick, where there was a short second siege followed by a surrender and a treaty. The Treaty of Limerick contained military and civil articles. The former allowed the Jacobite officers to leave for the continent in the great diaspora of the Old English known as the 'Flight of the Wild Geese'. The civil articles promised religious toleration; they were quickly dishonoured. The English conquest was complete.

16. ASCENDANCY

The long wars were over. Ireland was at peace because one side had achieved a decisive, overwhelming victory. The Protestant interest was everywhere secure, although the memory of its recent insecurities was strong enough to make it ungenerous and unyielding in its hour of triumph. King William and the English parliament would have been content to honour the civil articles of the Treaty of Limerick. It was the Irish parliament, with the memories of 1641 and 1688 still fresh in its mind, which refused to do so.

The Protestant Ascendancy of the 18th century consisted of major landowners who subscribed to the Church of Ireland, an Anglican church but one with a pronounced Calvinist streak which influenced its worship and liturgical practices, if not the secular behaviour of its members. The real Calvinists, though, were the Ulster Presbyterians (or Dissenters), a separate regional sub-group for whom the Ascendancy had little affection. The Ascendancy passed a series of penal laws against Catholics and Dissenters alike in the early years of the 18th century, of which those against the Catholics were more onerous. These were directed against Catholic

● *Castletown House, Co. Kildare. Completed in 1732, it is the best example of Palladian country house architecture in Ireland.*

ownership of land, already reduced to barely 10 per cent of the island, in the hope of further diminishing Catholic influence. In the 18th century, land ownership meant power. Catholics were also forbidden to practise law, to hold public office or to bear arms. Younger sons who conformed to the Church of Ireland could disinherit their older brothers who did not.

These acts were not part of a proselytising effort. Protestants had no desire to convert Catholics, simply to neutralise them in the public sphere. Despite formal prohibitions against the practice of Catholicism, there was little

● *James Gandon's masterpiece, the Custom House (1791), stands on the lower reaches of the River Liffey.*

● *The old library at Trinity College, designed by Thomas Burgh in 1712*

formal persecution. Indeed, the Catholic Church maintained its institutional structures in good order throughout the century. And it was a changed church, for under the impact of defeat, Catholics were now seen as, and saw themselves as, a single, coherent group. No longer did the distinction between Gael and Old English have any currency. Now Catholics were simply the dispossessed. The feeling of dispossession was a constant feature of Catholic life from this point forward. It took different forms as social and political circumstances changed, but its essential proposition remained unchanged: the land of Ireland had been stolen from its rightful owners and given to strangers whose title to it was morally illegitimate.

● *Above: the Four Courts, also designed by Gandon, was completed towards the end of the 18th century.*

● *The north side of Merrion Square, Dublin. Merrion Square was laid out in the 1770s and is perhaps the finest of Dublin's Georgian squares.*

The penal laws were not rigorously enforced, especially after the 1730s as Protestants grew more relaxed. Still, they left a poisonous memory for the future. In the short run, their effect on the Ulster Dissenters, who were excluded from public office and subjected to various forms of minor discrimination, was more pronounced. Many of them simply left for the congenial atmosphere of Puritan New England, to the benefit of what later became the United States.

● *The west front of Trinity College, which dates from 1759*

The second half of the 18th century was the golden age of the Ascendancy. No longer merely a nervous and defensive colonial elite, they left their mark on the land – and especially on its cities. Georgian Dublin, with its mixture of noble public buildings and wonderfully coherent streetscapes, was their masterpiece. It still stands, although much knocked about by latter-day vandals. It was a uniquely Irish variation on the great European theme of Classical architecture. In the turbulent 17th century, only one public building of note – the Royal Hospital (1684) – was put up. In the 18th, all the great building works of Classical Dublin were either completed or set in train. There was no more fitting symbol of the long years of peace.

All the surface splendour of Ascendancy Ireland could not conceal the general poverty and backwardness of the country. It was a remote, faraway corner of Europe. In effect, it was an English colonial frontier. The colonial elite controlled everything, but remained alien in race, religion and to a great extent in language, for the Irish language was still the vernacular in large parts of the island.

● *The Old Parliament House, Dublin, now the Bank of Ireland, was the seat of the Irish House of Commons and House of Lords prior to the 1800 Act of Union*

In theory, 18th-century Ireland was a separate kingdom sharing a common monarch with Great Britain. In reality, it was a colony and was governed as such. The colonial parliament was representative only of the Ascendancy interest and for most of the century remained hamstrung by ancient statutes like Poynings' Law of 1494, which made all Irish legislation subject to London's approval. These vexatious restrictions were removed in 1782, giving the Irish parliament formal independence. However, the real power in Ireland lay not with parliament but with the administration in Dublin Castle, which was dependent less on the support of the Irish parliament than on the confidence of the London government. The Castle was firmly in

the hands of an Ascendancy group which was both conservative and inflexible. John Fitzgibbon, who was Lord Chancellor of Ireland from 1789 until his death in 1802, was probably its key figure. He was coldly intelligent, able and every inch a realist. He kept in mind, above all else, the numerical weakness of the Ascendancy and drew the conclusion that liberal concessions – especially to Catholics – could only lead to ruin.

The question of concessions to Catholics emerged from the 1760s on. There were three reasons for this. First,

● *The Irish House of Commons in 1790*

● *One of the state rooms in Dublin Castle. In the 18th century, Dublin Castle was the true seat of power in Ireland.*

● *John Fitzgibbon, Lord Clare, Lord Chancellor of Ireland and probably the most influential of the Dublin Castle officials prior to the Act of Union*

serious agrarian unrest broke out in the countryside, as secret peasant societies organised campaigns of local terror and intimidation, often in opposition to agricultural reforms that threatened traditional employment patterns. Second, a reforming minority emerged among the Ascendancy, influenced by the liberal philosophies of the European Enlightenment. Third, the British government increasingly wished to see an end to the penal laws because it needed Irish Catholic recruits for the American War of Independence, for India, and later for the French revolutionary wars. Besides, the Irish Catholics had proved their reliability back in 1745 when the Scottish Jacobite rebellion under Bonny Prince Charlie found no echo there, although this was due not to anti-Jacobite hostility but to the effects of a severe famine in the early 1740s which claimed about 300,000 lives and left the Irish peasantry exhausted.

Under English pressure, the Irish parliament passed a Catholic Relief Act in 1778 which eased the restrictions on Catholic land ownership. The really radical measure came 15 years later, as the twin fears of the French wars and Irish unrest caused London to act over the heads of the protesting Ascendancy. Catholics were allowed to enter the professions, especially the law and the army, were given the vote on the same basis as Protestants, and were permitted to join militia companies and therefore to bear arms.

By the 1790s, the situation in Ireland was most unstable. Agrarian discontent had bred a plethora of violent secret societies and there was widespread unrest in the countryside. In Ulster, this had taken a sectarian turn, as the Protestant and Catholic lower orders clashed over employment and land. Out of this emerged the Orange Order, devoted to the traditional Protestant supremacy; and the Defenders, their Catholic mirror image. Both were sectarian populist movements; both stressed sectarian solidarity above all else. The Orange Order still exists. The Defenders have long since disappeared but Defenderism – the practice of Catholic communal solidarity – has not.

● *Henry Grattan, leader of the 'Patriot' opposition in the Irish House of Commons*

18. THE GATHERING STORM

Into this world of worsening agrarian and sectarian unrest, the French Revolution of 1789 burst like a firecracker. Its heady doctrines of liberty, democracy and the rights of man left nobody in Ireland untouched. It terrified the Ascendancy; it radicalised Protestant liberals; and it rekindled an old dream among Catholics.

Ever since 1691, there had been a persistent undercurrent among the Catholic dispossessed which longed for a Stuart restoration. It was a constant contained culture which resented the petty restrictions placed upon them by the Dublin Anglican elite. They were perhaps the most politically literate group in Ireland and French doctrines had a natural appeal to them, familiar as they were with their own democratic structures of church government.

In 1791, a group of Dissenters founded the Society of United Irishmen in Belfast. A Dublin society was founded shortly after. It was a radical pressure group for parliamentary reform. Many of its original objectives – less religious discrimination and wider manhood

To subvert the tyranny of our execrable government, to break the connection with England, the never failing source of all our political evils, and to assert the independence of our country: these were my objects.

Theobald Wolfe Tone,
Autobiography

● Wolfe Tone

● Bantry Bay, Co. Cork, where the French fleet lay at anchor but were unable to land in December 1796

feature of Irish-language poetry in the early 18th century. That hope died in 1745, but the dream of a foreign enemy of England which could deliver Irish Catholics from their bondage did not. In the 1790s, it focused anew on revolutionary France.

This was far removed from the world of the Ulster Dissenters, who were also deeply attracted to the French revolution, but for very different reasons. The Ulster Presbyterians had developed a sophisticated, self-

suffrage – were conceded in the Catholic Relief Act of 1793, but by then some of its leaders had been further radicalised under the continuing pressure of revolutionary events in France. These radicals sought to make Ireland a republic and break the connection with England. The most important person in this category was a young disaffected Protestant lawyer from Dublin: Theobald Wolfe Tone.

Tone is the father of Irish republicanism. He, more than anyone, turned the United Irishmen from a radical pressure group into a full-blown republican conspiracy. He was an out-and-out separatist who sought, as he wrote 'to substitute the common name of Irishman in place of the denominations of Protestant, Catholic and Dissenter'. A strange mixture of optimist, opportunist, idealist and innocent, Wolfe Tone is one of the most attractive characters in Irish history. In 1794, he was almost compromised by a French spy and was lucky to get away to America, whence he made his way to France. There he persuaded the French government to send a large invasion force to an Ireland which, he assured them, was ripe for revolution. It sailed in December 1796 but was held up by contrary winds as it rode at anchor in Bantry Bay, Co. Cork. Unable to land, the French returned home; the British government and the Dublin Castle administration breathed again. It had, however, been a very close shave.

The United Irishmen were the only non-sectarian force of any consequence in Ireland, although some of the Ulster Dissenters among them had inherited a dislike of popery that sat quite easily with French Revolutionary principles. In effect, the United Irishmen outside Ulster sought to place themselves at the head of the

● *This late-18th-century engraving of peasants cutting turf (or peat) illustrates the harshness of much Irish rural life.*

Catholic masses whose energies they hoped to harness to a revolutionary end. Ranged against them was the government, which now embarked on a policy of wholesale repression of the populace in the countryside. This was carried out by the army commander in Ireland, General Gerard Lake, a dull-minded but efficient brute. Spying and treachery also did their job and resulted in the capture and imprisonment of the Leinster leadership of the United Irishmen in March 1798.

This meant that the rebellion, when it came two months later, was deprived of those who sought to give it a national purpose. In their absence, older and more sinister forces were unleashed.

● *The Old Charitable Institute, Clifton House, Belfast, was built in a style which echoes that of colonial New England.*

19. REVOLUTION AND REACTION

The rebellion of 1798 broke out in Leinster on 23 May. It was a complex mixture. The widespread influence of French republican ideas gave it the character of a revolutionary war, which aimed to create an entirely new social order. But it was also in part an old-style rural revolt, seeking simply to avenge or correct injustices in the existing social structure. Ultimately, agrarian grievances mingled with hatred of the military and with traditional dreams of Catholic deliverance to make a highly volatile cocktail. The residual leadership of the United Irishmen was unable to control events. There was no national uprising. Counties Wexford, Wicklow and Kildare saw most of the fighting. A peasant army, well disciplined at first, swept through the area and captured the key towns of Enniscorthy and Wexford. But within a

● *The Battle of Vinegar Hill, above Enniscorthy, Co. Wexford, was the decisive defeat for the rebel forces.*

● *The town of Enniscorthy as seen from the top of Vinegar Hill*

month, the whole affair in Leinster was over. The rebels could not consolidate their early successes, nor could they spread the insurrection into the midlands or Munster. A rebellion initially rich in republican ideals soon degenerated into sectarian slaughter with horrible atrocities committed by both sides. In the end, General Lake routed the rebels at Vinegar Hill.

In the meantime, however, a very different outbreak had occurred in the north. The United Irishmen – mostly radical Presbyterians – rose briefly in the Ulster counties of Antrim and Down, although their numbers diminished as word filtered through of the sectarian turn things had taken in the south. The broad mass of Presbyterians, let alone Ulster Protestants in general, stood aside from the United men, who were always a regional minority even among their own community. They were strongest in counties Antrim and Down, significantly the two Ulster counties with the fewest Catholics.

Finally, there was a brief outbreak in the west in August. A small French army, under General Humbert, landed at Killala, Co. Mayo, and had a few initial successes before its inevitable defeat. Almost as a postscript, a second French expedition tried to land in Donegal in October. It was intercepted. One of those captured was Wolfe Tone,

● *St Catherine's Church, Thomas St, Dublin, near which Emmet was hanged*

● A 1798 memorial at 'Croppy's Acre' in Dublin marks the site of a massacre of rebels by Crown forces.

in the uniform of a French officer. He was brought to Dublin, convicted of treason and committed suicide rather than let the British hang him. Five years later, in 1803, there was a coda to the year of liberty, as Robert Emmet – another middle-class Protestant United Irishman – touched off a brief affray in Dublin that led a mob to murder a judge and brought Emmet to the scaffold.

About 30,000 people died in 1798, many of them in circumstances of the most savage brutality. The decent idealism of the United Irishmen had reaped an ugly harvest. There were older, more enduring passions at work in Ireland than the passion for republican liberty. Political life was now wholly focused on the animosity between Protestant and Catholic, with the Presbyterians of the north thoroughly frightened into the Protestant camp. Just as Defenderism overwhelmed secular republicanism in Wexford, the fiercely Protestant Orange Order overwhelmed it in Ulster.

The reaction to 1798 was swift and decisive. The Irish parliament was persuaded to vote for its own dissolution and, under the Act of Union of 1800, Ireland became a wholly integrated part of the United Kingdom. A proposal to couple the Union with Catholic emancipation – which would have given Catholics the right to sit in parliament – was blocked by George III who believed that such a measure would breach his coronation oath in which he had sworn to uphold the Protestant nature of the state. But it was this question which, twenty years on, was to fuel a movement that took Ireland by storm.

The movement was called the Catholic Association and its formation marked the effective junction between Catholicism and Irish nationalism. Its leader was Daniel O'Connell.

● Robert Emmet, leader of the abortive rising of 1803

● Oulart Hill, Co. Wexford, scene of a battle in 1798

20. THE RISE OF O'CONNELL

O'Connell took the raw material of Defenderism and turned it from a crude vehicle for violent rural protest into a national, populist political movement. It was an achievement unique in Europe: the genuine mobilisation of a mass democratic majority for a peaceful political purpose.

O'Connell was born in Co. Kerry in 1775, the son of a marginal Catholic aristocratic family which had maintained its prosperity through a mixture of silence and cunning, not to mention smuggling. He was an early beneficiary of the Catholic Relief Act, 1793, which permitted Catholics to practise at the

● Daniel O'Connell

bar. He duly became a lawyer. Discontented lawyers are the classic nation-making class: educated, frustrated, resentful of the old order but respectful of legal process. O'Connell, Gandhi, Mandela: it is a constant pattern.

O'Connell had been educated in France where he had seen some of the excesses of the Revolution, and at the King's Inns in Dublin where he was actually a member of a militia company raised to combat the 1798 insurgents. The two experiences left him with a lifelong disdain for political violence, not on principle, but because of his conviction of its waste and futility.

By 1823 O'Connell was a legendary lawyer but a frustrated politician. He was barred from membership of parliament because of his religion. He bent his energies to clearing this obstacle, judging it – correctly – as the key barrier to Catholic advancement. In 1823, he founded the Catholic Association. It seemed only the latest in a long line of such associations, worthy, middle class and far too respectable for its own good. But it was none of these things, for a year later O'Connell introduced the category of associate member of the Association at a subscription of a penny a month and brought the masses into politics.

This subscription was collected through the one organisation that had a network throughout all of Catholic Ireland, the Catholic Church. O'Connell introduced the priest into Irish politics, and if later generations could berate him for that, he could at least plead pressing necessity. It worked. The rent was collected throughout the country and a population which was among the poorest in Europe was mobilised politically. It was an intensely practical business. O'Connell was a visionary but not an idealist: his campaigns were always directed towards specific ends

● *The interior of an Irish country inn in the early 19th century. It was people such as these who, although disenfranchised, represented the backbone of O'Connell's political support.*

● *The coach service established by an Italian, Charles Bianconi, revolutionised public transport in the south of Ireland in the early 19th century. Here one of his long cars drops a passenger.*

● *Detail of an Orange Order waistcoat from the period in the early 19th century when the Orange Order was banned. Despite this prohibition, Irish Protestant support for the Order was strong: the waistcoats were worn in secret.*

and he himself was keenly aware of the realities of Irish life, even the ugly, sectarian realities.

This was most clearly seen in the Clare by-election of 1828. One of the members of parliament for Co. Clare, William Vesey Fitzgerald, was seeking re-election. He was a liberal Protestant, a long-standing supporter of Catholic emancipation, and a member of a family with roots going back centuries to the Fitzgeralds of Desmond. His re-election should have been a formality.

It was not. In a revolutionary decision, O'Connell himself decided to challenge Fitzgerald even though, as a Catholic, he would be barred from taking his seat in the event of victory. He ran a nakedly sectarian campaign – and he won. It was a victory for the sheer power of numbers but was also celebrated as a great symbolic Catholic triumph, after what had seemed centuries of defeat.

Catholic Ireland had found its champion. O'Connell's achievement was staggering. He had effectively invented the modern Irish nation by harnessing the inheritance of history to a practical end. He had given that nation a new politics – populist, functional, skilled in shady tactics – which it took to with unwholesome enthusiasm. From 1828 on, the story of Irish nationalism is effectively a long footnote to the achievement of its founding father.

21. CATHOLIC EMANCIPATION

The government bowed to the inevitable force of O'Connell's victory. To defuse a potentially violent situation in Ireland, it conceded Catholic emancipation. This meant that Catholics could sit as MPs at Westminster without having to subscribe to the Oath of Supremacy, which was offensive to them in conscience. In addition, a whole

● *A detail from a painting of the House of Commons in 1833. Daniel O'Connell is about to take his seat.*

series of state appointments from which they had been barred were now open to them. This reform, which had been talked of for a generation, had been achieved with stunning speed in the end. It was, however, a victory bought at considerable price.

In the first place, the government of Wellington and Peel decided to neutralise the broad mass of O'Connell's supporters by the simple expedient of disenfranchising them. The backbone of the Catholic Association's vote – not just in Clare but in earlier by-elections in which Protestant candidates endorsed by them had won – was the so-called 'Forty-Shilling Freeholders'. These were tenants whose life interest in either a house or land was valued at not less than forty shillings, or £2. The government now raised the franchise limit to valuations

of £10 or more, thus producing in an instant a wealthier and much more conservative electorate.

O'Connell acquiesced in the abandonment of his staunchest supporters, reckoning correctly that while this mean-spirited measure could be reversed in time, emancipation could not. Such a view was typical of O'Connell the realist. Equally typical was his resigned acceptance of the sectarian realities of Irish life. No bigot himself, he none the less recognised that religious bigotry was an unsavoury fact of life in Ireland which simply could not be wished away. He had mobilised one of the poorest and most remote populations in Europe. Not only did he rely on the votes of the Forty-Shilling Freeholders, he also looked to the sheer force of numbers of landless labourers and cottiers who were excluded from the franchise but to whom he was a hero, their deliverer: the Liberator.

The malignant legacy of the 17th and 18th centuries had been the increasing polarisation of Irish life between Catholic and Protestant. Everywhere outside Ulster, a

● *The tower of Carlow Cathedral, built in 1833. The cathedral is a good example of the wealth and confidence of the revived Catholic community in the first half of the 19th century.*

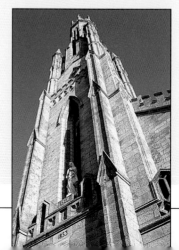

● A contemporary English cartoon opposing Catholic Emancipation. It shows Catholic 'hordes' being blown off course by the wind of Protestant truth. Note the scales of justice in which the crown and bible outweigh the papal tiara and rosary beads.

● Memorial to Archbishop James Warren Doyle of Kildare and Leighlin, the outstanding Catholic prelate in early 19th-century Ireland. He was a strong supporter of O'Connell.

● An early locomotive of the Dublin and Kingstown railway. The railway revolution was a most important social change in pre-famine Ireland.

I am the hired servant of Ireland, and I glory in my servitude.

Daniel O'Connell, letter

dispossessed Catholic majority faced a small Protestant elite. Not all Catholics were poor and marginalised, but most of them were. Not all Protestants were members of the ruling caste but even for those who were not, Protestantism was a badge of respectability and social superiority. The most effective forms of protest open to rural Catholics prior to O'Connell had been the agrarian secret societies which could at least settle local scores. Their methods were the rough expedients always resorted to by the excluded: violence, intimidation, sabotage. Their members were bound together by oaths and codes of silence and by the exclusion of strangers. Communal solidarity was the name of the game.

This was the only enduring tradition of populist organisation that preceded O'Connell and he tapped straight into it, overlaying it with the parish structure of the Catholic Church and stressing the one integrating element that bound the dispossessed together: their Catholicism. It was no accident that his great triumph in 1829 secured a specifically Catholic reform. Unlike the well-intentioned but frequently condescending Protestant republicans of the 1790s, O'Connell understood Irish Catholics, warts and all. He set the tone for Irish nationalism thereafter: overwhelmingly Catholic, strong on communal solidarity, populist, localist – and careful not to offend the priests.

22. REFORM AND REPEAL

After Catholic emancipation, O'Connell's formal objective was the repeal of the Act of Union that joined Ireland to England. However, there were specific short-term issues to be tackled and so he entered into a loose alliance with the Whig party, which was in government almost continuously from 1830 to 1841, but which had lost its overall parliamentary majority by 1835 and was glad of the support of the 60 or so MPs at O'Connell's disposal.

The principal benefit was the resolution of the tithes question. For more than a hundred years, the forced payment of tithes in support of the Church of Ireland had been a chronic source of complaint among Catholics. It had probably been the greatest single stimulus to the various rural secret societies. In the quickening political atmosphere following 1829, it became the main focus of popular discontent. The 'tithe war' of the 1830s was not pretty. Defenderism marched again, in the shape of murders, robberies, burnings, cattle-maimings and riots

● *The Rev. Henry Cooke, the dominant figure in Irish Presbyterianism in the first half of the 19th century, and an implacable opponent of O'Connell*

directed against the collection of tithes. Meanwhile, the state apparatus enforced payment by seizing the goods and produce of defaulters. It was not until 1838 that this running sore was finally remedied by legislation.

This and other reforms were, however, a far cry from the heroics of emancipation. Moreover, the big question of Repeal was effectively set aside for the period of the Whig alliance. Gradually, opposition to O'Connell grew among younger, radical elements in the Repeal Association who formed themselves into the Young Ireland movement. Influenced partly by the non-sectarian republicanism of the United Irishmen, partly by romantic German nationalism and partly by an impatience with O'Connell's parliamentary compromises, they were a generational reaction to his long domination of Irish life. Their

● *Memorial statue to Thomas Davis in College Green, Dublin. Davis was co-founder of* The Nation *newspaper and the most influential figure in the early Young Ireland movement.*

newspaper, *The Nation*, was extremely popular and their principal legacy was a propagandist one. They gave Irish nationalism much of its early poetry, symbolism and iconography. But in the short term, Young Ireland was a shambles achieving nothing except a tiny, bungled rebellion in 1848.

Before that, O'Connell had organised his last campaign. His parliamentary leverage gone with the return of the Tories in 1841, he launched a mass movement for Repeal of the Union, holding a series of 'monster meetings' at different venues. These venues did not, however, include Ulster, a province of which O'Connell was almost completely ignorant. He hardly ever visited it and his campaigns always faltered there in the face of stern Protestant opposition.

And it was a very different Protestantism from that which had provided the Ulster rebels of 1798. In 1829, the very year of Catholic emancipation, the liberal 'New Light' Presbyterians under the Rev. Henry Montgomery were routed at the church's general assembly by the more conservative forces of the Rev. Henry Cooke, a stern, anti-papist Calvinist of the old school, whose views set the tone of Ulster Presbyterianism for generations. Significantly, even the liberal Montgomery was as opposed

● *O'Connell Street, Dublin, the O'Connell monument in the foreground*

as Cooke to Repeal, both men equally fearing Catholic domination of a restored Irish parliament.

O'Connell's Repeal campaign eventually petered out in the face of firm government opposition and his inability to bring any effective pressure to bear on Westminster. By now he was ailing and his world was collapsing under the shattering effects of the Great Famine. He died in January 1847. He was a man great in his contradictions and complexities, by turns agitator, orator, compromiser, organiser. His faults as much as his virtues contributed to his creation: the modern Irish nation.

● *A monster meeting in Clifden, Co. Galway, in September 1843. O'Connell addresses the crowd in support of his Repeal campaign.*

23. THE FAMINE

In 1841, the first truly reliable census of Ireland revealed a population of 8,175,124 persons. This compared with an estimate of barely four million 40 years earlier. This teeming population, almost entirely rural and impoverished, was sustained by the potato, the staple food of the Irish peasantry. It was nutritional and produced exceptionally high yields. The huge increase in the population was encouraged by endless

● *A peasant cottage in south Leinster from* The Illustrated London News *of 1843, two years before the Famine*

● *A food riot in Dungarvan, Co. Waterford, as a desperate crowd fights to get in to a locked baker's premises. This drawing was first reproduced in* The Pictorial Times *on 10 October 1846.*

sub-division of holdings, which meant that more and more people were crowded on to ever tinier plots of land, all producing potatoes to sustain their swelling numbers. In 1841, almost two-thirds of all farms in Connacht were less than five acres in size. By 1845, the potato was the sole source of food for one-third of the Irish. There was little pressure to endure the hardships of emigration if one could subsist at home. Nor, outside eastern Ulster, was there any urban industrial revolution to absorb the surplus rural population.

In the autumn of 1845, about one-third of the potato crop failed. It was not an immediate disaster, for most people had something in reserve with which to buy food. Besides, this sort of thing had happened before. What was different was that this failure was caused by a new, unknown fungus and it spread throughout the country. There was much distress that winter which the Tory government of Sir Robert Peel tried to alleviate with shipments of Indian corn. In the summer of 1846, Peel's government fell to be replaced by the Whigs under Lord John Russell. They were much more doctrinaire in their attachment to the idea of *laissez faire*, believing that the state should not meddle in the economy, leaving market forces to determine the outcome of events instead.

In 1846, the crop failed again. Now terrible starvation began in earnest. The numbers of people employed on relief schemes of all sorts reached 500,000 by the end of the year and almost 750,000 by the spring of 1847. Soon, it was over a million. Yet, incredibly, the government insisted that such schemes be funded locally, not nationally. The burden was to fall upon the local ratepayers, in short, upon the landlords. But the landlords, many of whom belied their traditional reputation

● *The hideous conditions on board an emigrant ship travelling from Ireland to the United States in the mid 19th century*

● *Lord John Russell, Prime Minister of the United Kingdom for most of the Famine*

by foregoing rents, could not possibly bear such an enormous financial burden. Some landlords had no choice but to evict people for non-payment of rent, lest they themselves go under. Many did anyway. Thus there was the grotesque sight of tens of thousands of utterly destitute, starving people wandering around parts of Ireland while the British government – the richest in the world – refused to apply its resources directly to the problem.

Then came famine fever: typhus, dysentery, scurvy. Horror piled upon horror. The crop did not fail completely in 1847 but yields were very low, in part because seed potatoes had already been consumed by desperate people. The fungus returned in 1848 and not until the following year can it be said that the Famine was over. It was the last great subsistence crisis in Western Europe.

About a million people died. Another million fled overseas. It was a calamity on a scale so vast that it would have overwhelmed any government, even one disposed to deal sympathetically with the problem. The Whigs were not. They and their Treasury officials were ill-disposed to what they regarded as the irresponsible Irish, caught in a trap of their own making. *Laissez faire*, the economic theory that made Britain rich, had caused Ireland to starve. The question for the future was whether Ireland could ever be governed justly by British methods.

● *Above left: Sir Charles Trevelyan, Under-Secretary at the Treasury during the Famine*
● *Above right: Sir Robert Peel, former Chief Secretary of Ireland and Prime Minister in the first year of the Famine. His time in Ireland gave him an insight into the crisis that eluded his successors.*

24. THE IRISH DIASPORA

There had always been emigration from Ireland. Mercenary soldiers, disaffected Ulster Presbyterians, resourceful men willing to chance their arms in a wider world: the pattern was well established. It is the way with offshore islands. But the Famine emigration was different. It was wholesale flight, a human haemorrhage on a colossal scale. Impoverished, frightened and bitter people were prepared to pack into the steerage sections of boats, there to endure the horrors of a transatlantic voyage in cramped, ill-ventilated and insanitary conditions, rather than remain in Ireland.

Over 780,000 people went to the United States in the 1840s. Others went to Britain; a few adventurous souls risked the incredibly long journey to Australia, there to join their countrymen who had been banished down under at Her Majesty's pleasure. In the next

● Sean Keating's 'Economic Pressure', a graphic reminder of the prime reason for the massive Irish diaspora

Australia were too few and too far away. The Irish in Britain tended to be the least skilled or the poorest who could only afford the short cross-channel passage. The Irish in America, however, were numerous, homogeneous and ambitious – a force to reckon with.

Although from an overwhelmingly rural country, the Irish settled in the cities, especially those on the east coast. They had neither the capital reserves nor the sophisticated agricultural techniques to exploit the opportunities which the prairies afforded

● Now closed, the arrivals hall at Ellis Island, in New York harbour, once teemed with immigrants.

● A New York St Patrick's Day parade passing the reviewing stand at City Hall during the 1870s

decade, almost a million Irish emigrants arrived on the shores of America. Emigration was no longer just reaction to the cataclysm of the Famine; it had become a way of life. From 1850 to 1930, Irish emigration to America alone totalled over four million persons.

Of all the emigrant experiences, that in the United States was the most crucial for future Irish history. The Irish in

● *John F. Kennedy, 35th President of the United States, was the first Catholic in the office. His success mirrored that of the whole Irish-American community.*

The people have the liberty of voting, but we have the liberty of counting.

Remark attributed to a Tammany Hall politician

to Swedes, Norwegians and Germans. Moreover, they had two skills that stood them in good stead in the cities: the English language and a knowledge of rough political manoeuvring that they had learned from O'Connell.

Tammany Hall was the result. The Irish got a grip on big city government that was still capable of delivering the goods as late as 1960, when the last of such formidable Irish political machines – that of Mayor Richard Daley of Chicago – organised a classic ballot-stuffing exercise to win the state of Illinois and with it the Presidency of the United States for John F. Kennedy. The patronage system rewarded friends, punished enemies and, most importantly for those in Ireland contemplating emigration, ensured a steady supply of municipal employment for newly arrived Irish immigrants.

The Irish thus became one of the crucial elements in the Democratic party. They were rough but effective: as Franklin Roosevelt was to say of them, 'They may be sons of bitches but they are our sons of bitches.' And although America baulked at electing a Catholic of Irish extraction to the White House until 1960, the Irish influence was pervasive.

All this bore on things back home. The Irish in America carried in their hearts a burning hatred of Britain for what they held to be the genocidal policy of the Whigs during the Famine. Their support for militant nationalism, separatism and republicanism was always greater than in Ireland itself. But it meant that Britain now had a powerful, implacable and influential enemy within a country whose opinions were of increasing world importance. And nationalists in Ireland had a fruitful source of money, guns, dynamite and propaganda. They were soon to make their presence felt.

● *Ned Kelly, the famous Australian bushranger, came of an Irish family. Like many Irish-Australians, Kelly felt an outsider in his adopted country. This general alienation led the Irish to play a significant role in Australian politics through the Labour party and the trade union movement.*

The Young Ireland movement had represented, among other things, that strain in the Irish nationalist tradition that looked back beyond the populist Defenderism of O'Connell to the secular republicanism of 1798. Where O'Connell had always deprecated '98, the Young Irelanders celebrated it. In 1858, two Young Ireland veterans – James Stephens and John O'Mahony – founded the Irish Republican Brotherhood. Stephens had spent most of the 1850s in Paris before returning to Ireland; O'Mahony was still based in New York. The IRB was therefore a transatlantic organisation.

Its nickname, the Fenians, came from the *Fianna*, legendary warriors of Celtic Ireland. The Fenians were out-and-out militants, seeking to secure an Irish republic through force of arms and through no other means. They combined radical republicanism with a kind of latter-day Defenderism, uniting old and new forms of Irish militancy. It was a potent, if unstable, mixture.

Stephens organised the Fenians in Ireland along the lines of the French revolutionary movements he had experienced in Paris. This, however, brought him into conflict with the one organisation in nationalist Ireland that mattered more than any other: the Catholic Church. The days of the penal laws long behind it, the Church was powerful, ubiquitous and supremely self-confident. Its formidable leader, Paul Cardinal Cullen, archbishop of

● *Fighting in front of St Malachy's Catholic Church in 1864. From the 1850s onward, there was a pattern of vicious sectarian rioting in Belfast, as the ancient quarrels of the countryside came to the town.*

● *Above left: James Stephens, leader of the Fenians prior to the rising of 1867*
● *Above right: Paul Cardinal Cullen, the outstanding figure in the Catholic Church in 19th-century Ireland. An ultramontane, he was responsible for the reorganisation of the Church following the Great Famine.*

Dublin, had been for many years an influential figure in Rome, where he had acquired a hatred of revolutionary conspiracy as great as Stephens' love of it. The enmity of the Church merely reinforced the minority standing of republican conspiracy within the overall Irish nationalist tradition.

Stephens was a vain and incompetent leader who promised rebellion but could deliver nothing better than an attempt in 1867 that was scarcely less farcical than the Young Ireland fiasco 19 years earlier. But the Fenian tradition lived on, partly in song

and story, partly in the fanaticism of dynamite terrorists who maintained a campaign in Britain in the 1880s similar to the modern IRA campaign. Always a minority, always simon-pure, often mocked, the Fenians would have the last laugh yet.

None of this meant a thing in Protestant Ulster. For there, as if to

● The results of a Fenian bomb in the House of Commons in 1885. The Fenians ran a sporadic campaign of dynamiting British targets in the 1880s.

overlay the deadly historical inheritance of settler and native, the industrial revolution took off. While most of Ireland starved in the 1840s, north-east Ulster roared ahead. Linen mills, shipyards and engineering expanded at a phenomenal rate. Belfast grew from a small provincial town to a booming city, to which thousands of poor country people flocked in search of work.

Ulster's industrial revolution was a Protestant phenomenon – and

● The plundering of McConvill's spirits stores and the looting of shops during more sectarian riots in Belfast in 1872

specifically a Presbyterian one. A well-established education system and the Calvinist work ethic combined to make Protestant Ulster not just rich but self-consciously part of a greater British prosperity. The industrial revolution bound Protestant Ulster to the Union. It also created a large urban working-class, especially in Belfast. This was composed of both Protestants and Catholics, although Protestants more often held the skilled jobs. Both groups brought with them their malign histories. As early as the 1850s the pattern of sectarian rioting had moved from countryside to town and especially to Belfast. A long fuse had been lit.

26. LAND AND NATION

After the trauma of the Famine, nationalist Ireland was exhausted. There was no successor to O'Connell. The Fenians revived and reinterpreted militant, romantic republicanism but they were always a minority, albeit an important one. Not until the 1870s does the tradition of populist nationalism re-assert itself.

A campaign to re-establish an Irish parliament which would control domestic affairs was started in 1870 under the leadership of a Protestant barrister called Isaac Butt. It was not separatist, but federalist. It sought home rule for Ireland within the United Kingdom. It looked back more to the Protestant 'Patriots' of the old Irish parliament than to O'Connell. But it still drew Catholic support. By the late 1870s, the Home Rulers had 56 MPs at Westminster. They soon wearied of Butt, an ineffectual leader, dropping him in favour of the most enigmatic figure in Irish history: Charles Stewart Parnell.

Parnell came from an unlikely background – that of a long-established Protestant landlord family in Co. Wicklow. He was chilly, remote, formidable and utterly ruthless. By the mid-1880s he had transformed the Home Rulers into the Irish Parliamentary Party. It built a national constituency organisation throughout Ireland; its parliamentary candidates were bound by a degree of internal discipline as yet unknown in either of the major British parties, complete with whips and binding pledges to support

● *Below: Mr Walter Burke, a West of Ireland landlord, serves a writ on one of his tenants.*
● *Bottom: the arrest of William O'Brien MP and John Dillon MP outside the Land League offices in Loughrea, Co. Galway, during the Land League agitation*

● *Parnell*

party policy unswervingly; and it was quite happy to filibuster its way to the attention of parliament without any concern for manners or tradition.

The IPP also contained members who were closer to the Fenians than one might expect in parliamentarians. It was through Fenian contacts that Parnell first became involved with the Irish National Land League, which he founded with Michael Davitt in 1879.

● *Michael Davitt, co-founder of the Irish National Land League*

● *A western eviction scene from the 1880s. The consequence of eviction for non-payment of rent was an empty house and a homeless family. Such a scene had a powerful effect on the nationalist imagination.*

Davitt was the polar opposite of Parnell, the son of a Co. Mayo tenant farmer who had been evicted in 1850. The Land League had three aims: fair rent, fixity of tenure and free sale of a tenant's interest in a property. The land war of the 1880s was, in many respects, the revival of an old tradition of agrarian violence. Now, however, it was specifically focused on land reforms that were so far-reaching they could only be accomplished by political means. Two great issues were joined : who was to own the land of Ireland and

who was to govern the land of Ireland? All through the decade, the land war went on in one form or another. Boycotts, arson, cattle-maiming, intimidation: all the traditional techniques were employed against landlords and their agents. The government in London reacted with a mixture of coercion and conciliation. The 1881 Land Act established the principle of the tenant's interest in his holding and set up arbitration courts to settle rent and other disputes. The 1885 Act accelerated the process of actual land purchase by making loans available on easy terms to tenants who wished to buy. The process of facilitating tenant purchase eventually matured fully in the Land Act of 1903, which effected the transfer of huge tracts of land from landlords to tenants. It replaced the old landed Ascendancy with the network of small, independent proprietors which exists today. The Cromwellian confiscations were undone and a system that had always lacked moral legitimacy was finally swept away.

The new owners were not, of course, the descendants of those dispossessed in the 17th century. Ireland had changed far too much for that, but none the less, the land settlement was seen as the righting of a great historical wrong.

27. THE UNCROWNED KING

Parnell's alliance with Davitt brought the Irish land question to the floor of the House of Commons in the most urgent way possible. As with ownership of land, so with the governing of Ireland. Home Rule first became an urgent issue in British political life after the 1885 general election which returned 85 IPP (or Nationalist) MPs to give Parnell the balance of power. He used it to force the British Prime Minister's hand.

Gladstone introduced a Home Rule bill in 1886, which split his Liberal party and was defeated. The government fell. No matter, though, Home Rule for Ireland was now on the British political

● *Katharine (Kitty) O'Shea*

● *Above left: Gladstone introducing the first Home Rule Bill in the House of Commons, 1886*
● *Above right: Parnell addressing a political meeting in Cork in the mid 1880s*

agenda. The Tories were pledged to oppose it in perpetuity but the majority of the Liberals who had stayed with Gladstone in 1886 were committed to an alliance with Parnell. It seemed to the Irish only a matter of time before the natural pendular motion of the British two-party system would return the Liberals to power and then the battle could be joined again. Parnell was all-powerful in Ireland. He had built a political organisation more formidable and disciplined than O'Connell's, although owing much to that organiser

of genius; he was well on the way to solving the land problem; he had the Catholic Church on his side, a *sine qua non* for any Irish nationalist leader; and the people adored him. He was the 'uncrowned king of Ireland'.

There was just one fly in the ointment: Ulster. Parnell knew as little of the north as had O'Connell. Nor was his Protestantism any help, for he was a very indifferent Anglican with no liking for the ardent Calvinism of the Ulster chapels. The 1886 Home Rule bill had galvanised Protestant Ulster. Suddenly aware of the threat to the Union, they were the main force behind the formation of the Irish Unionist Party in 1886. Ulster was the only area which returned Unionists to Westminster in concentrated numbers at the election that followed the fall of Gladstone's government. Protestant Ulster was as resistant to nationalist penetration as it had ever been. It would remain so.

Yet it was not Ulster that broke Parnell, but a sexual scandal. He had for years been living with Mrs Katharine O'Shea, the estranged wife of one his own Nationalist Party colleagues, Capt. William O'Shea, a feckless and improvident philanderer. O'Shea eventually sued for divorce in 1890,

● Irish MPs (above) frequently created disturbances in the House of Commons by filibustering and otherwise interrupting regular proceedings to get Irish grievances recognised.

> *No man has the right to fix the boundary to the march of a nation. No man has the right to say: "Thus far shalt thou go and no further".*
>
> **Charles Stewart Parnell**

citing Parnell as co-respondent, and was granted a decree. At first little happened; then the lid blew off the pot. First Gladstone, under pressure from his own backbenchers, distanced himself from Parnell; then, fatally, the Irish Catholic hierarchy turned against 'the adulterer'. Parnell's leadership of the IPP was challenged. Nationalist MPs were caught in a horrible dilemma. Should they remain loyal to the Liberal alliance, which alone could deliver Home Rule, and to the Catholic bishops who wielded such immense moral authority back home? Or should they stay with Parnell, who had brought them to the mountain top?

They chose the Liberals and the bishops in what was probably the

● *Below: following the Parnell split, there was a series of bitter by-elections, one of them in North Kilkenny. Here Parnell is attacked by a hostile crowd while leaving Castlecomer.*

bitterest split in Irish political history. Parnell fell. He tried to recover ground by fighting a series of by-elections in Ireland which were contested with a vituperation and a viciousness never seen before or since. He failed. Never in robust health, he died in Katharine's arms in October 1891. He was 45. His fall was like something from Greek tragedy and it poisoned the life of nationalist Ireland for a generation.

● *The Parnell memorial at the intersection of O'Connell Street and Parnell Street, Dublin. The quote is from a speech which Parnell made in Cork in 1884.*

The fall of Parnell coincided with what is usually called the cultural revival in nationalist Ireland. Just as politics and the land question had quickened in the 1880s, so did the other elements which contributed to the birth of the modern Irish state 40 years later. A nationalist middle class formed. A movement for the revival of the ancient Irish (or Gaelic) language got under way. There was a burgeoning literary movement which saw a great flowering of poetry, drama and fiction. The study of Irish history took on a new urgency.

At a popular level, a most important organisation was founded in Thurles, Co. Tipperary, in 1884. The Gaelic Athletic Association (GAA) promoted native Irish sports, especially Gaelic football and the ancient game of hurling. It achieved an astonishing popularity and was soon established in every parish in nationalist Ireland. One must write 'nationalist Ireland', for the GAA was from the start aggressive in its nationalism, and contained Fenians and Fenian sympathisers among its leading figures. It was unlike the Fenians in that it was genuinely popular, but like them in its radical politics and also in its conspiratorial suspicion of outsiders. From early years, it placed a ban on persons who played what it defined as 'foreign' games – soccer, rugby, hockey and cricket. To play or even attend one of these games was to ensure exclusion from the GAA. It was no organisation for unionists or, indeed, for those nationalists who thought of themselves as respectable middle-class gentlemen.

The latter were increasingly dominant in the IPP, reunited in 1900 following the Parnell split, and now under the leadership of John Redmond. Nobody paid much attention to a nationalist ginger group called Sinn Fein which was founded by a Dublin journalist, Arthur Griffith, in 1905. The

● *A view of Ewart's factory in Belfast in the late 19th century. Factories such as this lay at the heart of Ulster prosperity.*

● *A modern hurling match between Cork and Tipperary. The Gaelic Athletic Association, founded in 1884, is perhaps the most important popular cultural movement in modern Ireland.*

● *At the final demonstration of Unionist protest outside the Ulster Hall on the eve of the signing of the Ulster Solemn League and Covenant, Sir Edward Carson waves the flag carried before William III at the Battle of the Boyne.*

● *A parade of National Volunteers in Co. Sligo, 1914*

early Sinn Fein was not republican. It wanted Irish MPs to abstain from attending Westminster and instead to form themselves into a constituent assembly in Dublin with the intention of achieving a kind of dual monarchy solution along the lines of the Austro-Hungarian empire. But Redmond, not Griffith, seemed the man of the hour. His moment came in 1910 when he found himself holding the balance of power in parliament, as Parnell had 25 years before. He did as the master had done, trading a Home Rule bill in return for IPP support for a Liberal government.

Eventually, the Home Rule bill of 1912 came before the House of Commons. Its prospects for success looked good, so good that it produced a violent reaction among the Ulster Protestants. Under the leadership of Edward Carson – a Dubliner – and

● *Sir James Craig, later Lord Craigavon, Ulster Unionist leader and first Prime Minister of Northern Ireland*

● *Arthur Griffith and E.J. Duggan, signatories of the Anglo-Irish treaty of December 1921. Griffith (left) was the original founder of Sinn Fein.*

James Craig, a huge popular mobilisation took place. A 'Solemn League and Covenant' against Home Rule – a very Calvinist thing, this, with consciously Biblical echoes of God's covenant with the children of Israel – was signed by over 400,000 Ulstermen. They did not stop at that. They organised the outlines of a provisional government, pledged to defy the implementation of Home Rule. They imported arms illegally. British army officers stationed at the Curragh, Co. Kildare, refused to march against them. Leading figures in British Conservative politics colluded with them in an extraordinary exhibition of treason in defence of the Union.

The Home Rule bill was passed by parliament in September 1914, by which time Europe was at war. Operation of the bill was suspended for the duration of the conflict. In the meantime, Irishmen of all political hues went into battle. Nationalists fought for the rights of small nations; unionists for the empire. At least 35,000 died. Those who survived returned to an Ireland transformed.

When the Great War broke out, Redmond pledged the support of nationalist Ireland to the British war effort. What else could he do, with Home Rule already in the bag, without appearing treacherous? But this decision split the Irish Volunteers, a recently formed nationalist militia group. Those who followed Redmond called themselves National Volunteers. The dissenting minority retained the old name.

The Irish Volunteers were effectively separatists of one kind or another. And secreted away within this minority was another minority, more separatist than all the rest: the IRB. The Fenians were back. Under the leadership of Thomas J. Clarke, Sean MacDermott and Patrick Pearse, they planned an armed insurrection while Britain was at war. They sent emissaries to Germany in search of arms and support against the common enemy. They took the militant socialist, James Connolly, and his tiny Irish Citizen Army, into their confidence. They kept the formal leadership of the Irish Volunteers completely in the dark about their plans. On Easter Monday, 24 April 1916, they seized a number of public buildings in the centre of Dublin. On the roof of one of them, the General Post Office in O'Connell St, they hoisted the tricolour of the Irish Republic, while Patrick Pearse stood at the front door below and read out the proclamation of the Republic of Ireland.

The proclamation appealed to a seamless tradition of nationalist revolt which encompassed the Fenians, the Young Irelanders, Robert Emmet and 1798. This rather unpromising series of precedents – three farces and a tragedy – represented a very partial reading of Irish history but it provided the rising with a plausible and emotionally resonant pedigree. Furthermore, the rising itself was neither a tragedy nor a farce. While it only lasted a week, the Volunteers fought cleanly and honourably. In the course of suppressing it, the British sailed a

● *The General Post Office, (GPO) Dublin, headquarters of the 1916 Easter Rising*

● *Below: Patrick Pearse*
● *Below right: Banna Strand, Co. Kerry, where Roger Casement's attempted landing of German arms was foiled just before the Easter Rising*

● Portraits of the seven signatories of the Proclamation of the Republic together with a copy of the Proclamation

● Oliver Shepherd's statue of the legendary Cuchulainn inside the GPO symbolises the spirit of sacrifice of the Easter Rising.

gunboat up the Liffey and devastated parts of the city centre. When it was all over, they executed 16 of the leaders.

From the British point of view, it was perfectly logical. The leaders had, after all, looked to Britain's enemy in the middle of a war. In case anyone had missed the point, the proclamation had referred to 'gallant allies in Europe'. But still, the executions were an act of folly and one against which the British were warned by many in a position to know. Redmond and his deputy, John Dillon, were especially vociferous. Bernard Shaw denounced the executions. So did the bishop of Limerick, a significant event given the Catholic Church's long and bitter hostility to the Fenians. Most of all, the executions gave Irish nationalism new martyrs – ones, moreover, who were to be celebrated in everything from popular ballads to some of W.B. Yeats's greatest poetry.

A nation needs poetry, heroes, great men and women. It needs these things in order to validate itself and to furnish it with the sense of pride and purpose that alone can sustain its independent existence. This is what the dead men of 1916 bequeathed to the Irish nation. The rising may have been an undemocratic revolutionary putsch, but all that was forgotten. What was remembered were the martyrs. Pearse's head and shoulders' portrait hung like an icon in thousands of Irish houses for at least two generations after that fateful Easter. He became the *beau ideal* of the new Ireland: a teacher, a poet, deeply religious with a mystic's gentle countenance.

Yeats was right when he wrote that 'all was changed, changed utterly'. The 1916 rising, and especially the executions, further weakened the ever-declining legitimacy of British rule in nationalist Ireland. The scene was set for revolution.

30. REVOLUTION AND CIVIL WAR

The British mistakenly blamed Sinn Fein for the rising and the political movement born out of the ashes took the Sinn Fein name. The leadership passed from Arthur Griffith to Eamon de Valera, the senior surviving commandant of 1916. The British now made another monumental blunder, threatening to introduce conscription in Ireland to replace the haemorrhage of men on the Western Front. (Significantly, Ireland had been exempted from previous conscription orders.) The threat was never carried out, but it was enough to unite all of nationalist Ireland – IPP, Sinn Fein, GAA, IRB and the Catholic Church – in bitter opposition. Naturally, as the most radically nationalist party, the anti-conscription campaign played into Sinn Fein's hands.

When the Great War ended in November 1918, there was a general election. In the heartland of Protestant Ulster, the Unionist vote held as solid as ever. Outside Ulster, Sinn Fein swept the old Nationalist party aside, winning 73 seats to their six. Sinn Fein acted on its old abstentionist beliefs and instead of attending Westminster, its elected members constituted themselves as Dail Eireann (the assembly of Ireland) and met in Dublin for the first time on 21 January 1919.

Think: what have I got for Ireland? Something she has wanted these past seven hundred years. Will anyone be satisfied with the bargain? Will anyone? I tell you this – early this morning I signed my death warrant. I thought at the time how odd, how ridiculous – a bullet may just as well have done the job five years ago.

Michael Collins, in a letter written after he had signed the Anglo-Irish Treaty

● *Michael Collins, Director of Organisation and Intelligence for the Irish Volunteers (later the IRA). A brilliant tactician, he was the dominating personality among the nationalists during the War of Independence. Tragically, he was assassinated during the civil war.*

● *A British barricade in Dublin, 1920*

● *Eamon de Valera, leader of Sinn Fein, inspects a detachment of men from the Western Division of the IRA in 1920.*

On the same day, the war of independence began as two Irish Volunteers shot two policemen in Co. Tipperary. The Volunteers, now called the Irish Republican Army (IRA), fought a sporadic campaign against crown forces for the next two and a half years. It mixed heroism and terrorism in equal measure. It was orchestrated by a brilliant young Corkman, Michael Collins, barely 30 years old, who infiltrated and smashed the British intelligence structure in Ireland. The British responded by unleashing armed and undisciplined auxiliary policemen, known as the Black and Tans, who terrorised the civilian population and were responsible for little more than arson and murder.

● British 'Black and Tans' frisking civilian suspects in Dublin in 1920

● The attack on the Four Courts by Free State troops began the short but vicious Irish civil war which followed the signing of the Anglo-Irish Treaty of 1921

Meanwhile, the island had been partitioned. The British bowed to the inevitable, recognised the unyielding opposition of the Ulster Protestants to even the slightest accommodation with nationalist Ireland and, with delicious irony, gave Home Rule within the UK to those who had originally least wanted it: the six most Protestant counties of the north-east. The southern unionists were sold down the river; the northern nationalists were trapped in an Orange state. The Ulster unionists had played the power game brilliantly and they had won.

In the south, the war of independence was still raging. Large parts of the country were effectively controlled by Sinn Fein who ran an alternative civil administration, complete with courts and police. There was eventually a truce followed by the Anglo-Irish treaty of December 1921. The chief negotiators for Sinn Fein were Arthur Griffith and Michael Collins. De Valera did not participate. And when the negotiators returned from London with dominion status for the 26 counties – effectively independence but not a republic – de Valera repudiated the agreement.

This division reflected a fundamental ambiguity in Sinn Fein's aims, for while it was a separatist party it was not a unanimously republican one, especially since it had displaced the Nationalists and was now obliged to represent a much broader coalition of interests than it had a few years earlier. Dail and people supported the settlement. Sinn Fein and the IRA split and a short, nasty civil war followed which claimed the lives of both Griffith and Collins. The pro-treaty side won. The new state was established. The Union Jack was lowered from Dublin Castle for the last time. In its place was hoisted the tricolour of Ireland free.

31. STATES OF IRELAND

Partition recognised an historical reality. The line of partition lay at the effective margin of British conquest. Only in Ulster was there a concentrated population which felt itself British by ties of blood, history, religion and allegiance. That population took as much of the historic province for itself as it could hold securely. The rest of Ireland became the Irish Free State,

● *Leinster House, Dublin, from Leinster Lawn, the seat of the Irish parliament*

● *Sir John Lavery's painting of a 12th July march in Portadown in the 1920s*

● *O'Connell Street, Dublin, in the 1940s*

corresponding to that part of the island which had remained Catholic at the Reformation. The Irish Free State gradually mutated into the Republic of Ireland, a process that was completed in 1949. Its politics were dominated first by William Cosgrave, who took over the reins after the deaths of Griffith and Collins, and later more thoroughly by Eamon de Valera. After ten years in the wilderness following the civil war, he formed his first government in 1932.

The party that de Valera founded, Fianna Fail, was in the grand tradition of O'Connell and Parnell in being a national, populist party with an organisational presence in every parish in the country. It has dominated the politics of the Republic since its foundation. For the first 40 years, the new state was principally concerned to express its differences from Britain and to guarantee its independence. It achieved the latter aim in the most unambiguous way by remaining neutral during World War II. De Valera's social vision was of a rural population, relatively insulated from urban modernity, speaking a revived Gaelic language. (The hoped-for revival has not happened.) This Jeffersonian vision was widely shared by the people and – most significantly – by an intensely conservative Catholic Church, which liked the idea of Ireland as a spiritual oasis in the material world.

Independent Ireland was cloyingly conformist. But it was an organic world,

● *A terrace of houses off the Falls Road, in the Catholic area of West Belfast, before the outbreak of the Troubles*

● Eamon de Valera, the dominant political personality in independent Ireland until his retirement in 1959

● An Irish classroom in the 1940s. Education in independent Ireland was dominated by priests and nuns.

at ease with itself. Economically, it was protectionist, attempting to build up Irish enterprises behind tariff walls, a strategy that worked in the short run but led to featherbedding, inefficiency and near economic collapse by the late 1950s. However, for all its faults, the independent Irish state was a pearl of great price: it had political legitimacy in the eyes of its people, something that had not existed in Ireland for centuries.

The Catholic triumph in the south was so total that it settled the historical quarrel for keeps and made the assimilation of the small Protestant minority relatively painless. But in the north, the unionists comprised merely 60% of the total population and the nationalists dreamed of reversing the partition settlement some day. They now looked to Dublin to deliver them as their ancestors had looked to France or Spain, but with a similar lack of results. The unionists reacted by emphasising the least generous features of the Irish Protestant tradition: a siege mentality; overt discrimination in jobs and public housing; and the effective reduction of northern Catholics to the rank of second-class citizens. The inheritance of Orangemen and Defenders, of communal solidarity and no surrender, was actually a rational if unwholesome response to the realities of Ulster life.

The Protestant province had almost 50 years of nervous but complacent ease. As part of the UK, it was materially better off than the south. The roads were better, the towns were more brightly lit at night, the countryside was neater and more carefully husbanded. To cross the border from north to south was to pass from an obviously cultivated landscape to a relatively neglected one, from a land that had been settled to one that had merely been colonised. But still, the Protestant north was chronically insecure – secretly terrified of the enemy within. Its terror was soon justified.

● William T. Cosgrave, the first President of the Executive Council (Prime Minister) of an independent Irish state following the end of the civil war. He was displaced by Eamon de Valera in 1932.

The 1960s shook north and south alike. The Republic, thoroughly frightened by the huge-scale emigration of the 1950s, abandoned protectionism, opted for free trade, attempted to join the European Community – doing so in 1972 – and generally tried to modernise by orientating itself much more towards the outside world.

● *Unionist hostility to the Anglo-Irish Agreement of 1985 was unrelenting. This huge crowd assembled in protest at Belfast City Hall on the first anniversary of the signing of the Agreement.*

● *The modern Republic remains a country torn between traditional Catholicism and secular liberalism. The 1984 referendum to continue to outlaw abortion was a victory for traditionalists.*

All this was the work of a new, well-educated middle class. They dreamed of Ireland as a European country much like any other, wealthy, urbanised and rid of ancient passions. Such people have dominated, some would say overwhelmed, the media, academic life and other sources of opinion formation. But they remain a minority in the population as a whole. The majority is more ambiguous about that kind of European modernisation, because there is only a weak tradition of civil society in nationalist Ireland. There is a strong sense of the nation but a weak sense of the state, except as a dispenser of patronage and welfare.

However, all these things were overshadowed by the outbreak of the Northern Ireland troubles in October 1968. A civil rights campaign sought such reforms as the allocation of public housing by need rather than sectarian preference, an end to electoral discrimination, and the dismantling of the spectacularly oppressive state security apparatus. The demands were resisted by most Protestants, who saw civil rights as a smokescreen for nationalism. Civil rights meetings ended in violence, some at the hands of the police and some at the hands of Protestant mobs. Before long, the initiative on the Protestant side passed to the ultras, of whom the Rev. Ian Paisley was the most charismatic. The latest in a malignant succession of bellowing, evangelical Ulster clerics, Paisley was never respectable – even among his own people, many regarded him with genteel horror – but he articulated Protestant defiance as no one else could.

By the summer of 1969, the situation had collapsed into wholesale violence. Urban working-class Catholics, first in Derry and then in Belfast, effectively rebelled against the police and the state

● *Garret FitzGerald, the Irish Taoiseach, and Margaret Thatcher, the British Prime Minister, sign the Anglo-Irish Agreement of 1985. By giving the Republic an input into the administration of policy in Northern Ireland, the Agreement infuriated northern Unionists.*

● *Mary Robinson, the first woman President of the Republic of Ireland*

● *An IRA firing party fires over the coffin of hunger striker Joe McDonnell in 1981. McDonnell was one of ten republican paramilitaries who died in hunger strikes that made international headlines but failed to force any major policy changes from the British government.*

itself. The sovereign power, Britain, was reluctantly dragged into the quagmire and the British army deployed to keep the sides apart. The IRA, long dormant, revived as a defensive militia for the Catholic ghettos. But faced with the old imperial enemy, it soon moved beyond defence to a campaign of terror designed to force a complete British withdrawal from Northern Ireland.

The past quarter century has brought significant changes in Northern Ireland. Most of the original civil rights demands have long since been met; the Belfast parliament was closed down by the British who now rule direct from London; an attempt at an internal power-sharing settlement collapsed under the weight of general Protestant disapproval; an Anglo-Irish agreement, which gives Dublin an input into Northern Ireland affairs, has survived intense Protestant hostility. For nearly twenty-five years, a vicious campaign of terrorism was conducted by the IRA until the declaration of a ceasefire in 1994. The effects of the violence were almost totally negative. The two communities have grown ever further apart. Indeed,

Northern Ireland is effectively an apartheid society: separate schools, separate churches, separate housing areas. There is no meeting of minds.

But if Northern Ireland is chronically unstable, the Republic at least can look back on 70 years of independence with pride and hope. The positive side of life in the south is personified by the President of the Republic, Mary Robinson. That a person of such obvious quality should be the first citizen of an independent Irish state seems all the more gratifying when one recalls the many dark corners and tragic moments in the long history of Ireland.

INDEX

ACKNOWLEDGEMENTS

British Museum, London p15 (top right)

Cork Public Museum, Cork p16 (bottom right)

Crawford Municipal Art Gallery, Cork p52 (top right)

G.A. Duncan p63 (top); p64 (bottom left); p67 (centre and bottom)

Gill and Macmillan, Dublin cover: bottom right; p60 (bottom left); p64 (bottom right)

Hulton Deutsch Collection, London cover: centre left; p35 (top); p43 (centre); p50 (both pics); p51 (left oval); p55 (bottom); p57 (top); p58 (centre left); p 61 (centre)

Irish Tourist Board, Dublin cover: top right; bottom left; p12 (top); p20 (centre left); p23 (centre right); p42 (centre); p62 (bottom right)

Mansell Collection, London p25 (centre); p27 (bottom); p31 (top left); p47 (top left); p59 (top right)

Mary Evans Picture Library, London cover: centre left; p19 (top right); p20 (bottom right); p21 (top); p22 (top); p23 (left oval); p25 (bottom); p26 (all pics); p30 (top); p32 (all pics); p33 (right oval); p34 (top); p39 (both pics); p40 (bottom); p51 (top right and right oval); p54 (top); p55 (centre right); p56 (centre left and bottom right); p57 (centre left); p59 (top left); p60 (bottom right); p64 (centre left); p65 (both pics); p67 (top)

Michael Diggin Photography, Tralee cover: centre right (b/w); p13 (bottom); p15 (left and bottom); p15 (centre right); p16 (right); p18 (bottom); p19 (centre right); p21 (centre); p30 (centre); p40 (centre); p43 (bottom); p47 (top right)

National Gallery of Ireland, Dublin p18 (top); p34 (bottom)

National Library of Ireland, Dublin p22 (bottom); p23 (right oval); p28 (centre left); p29 (bottom and centre); p31 (top right); p33 (left oval); p38 (centre right); p41 (top); p42 (top); p44; p45 (top and centre left); p47 (centre right); p49 (bottom); p54 (ovals); p58 (top and centre right); p60 (top); p61 (top); p62 (bottom left)

National Museum of Ireland, Dublin p9 (top left and centre); p11 (top left); p13 (top); p19 (bottom)

National Portrait Gallery, London p46 (top)

Office of Public Works, Dublin p29 (top left)

The Slide File, Dublin title page; introduction; p 6 (bottom); p7 (top left); p8 (top); p10 (top); p11 (bottom); p14 (bottom); p16 (top); p17 (left); p19 (centre left); p20 (bottom left); p24 (bottom); p25 (top); p31 (bottom right); p33 (bottom); p35 (top); p36 (top); p41 (bottom); p42 (bottom); p46 (bottom); p49 (top); p63 (bottom)

Derek Speirs/Report, Dublin all photographs on pp 68,69

Trinity College Dublin p10 (bottom left)

Ulster Museum, Belfast p45 (centre right); p48 (top); p51 (top left); p61 (bottom); p66 (top left)